TRANSNATIONAL BUSINESS AND CORPORATE CULTURE

PROBLEMS AND OPPORTUNITIES

edited by
STUART BRUCHEY
ALLAN NEVINS PROFESSOR EMERITUS
COLUMBIA UNIVERSITY

A GARLAND SERIES

TRANSCULTURAL CUSTOMIZATION OF INTERNATIONAL TRAINING PROGRAMS

HYUNJOO KIM

GARLAND PUBLISHING, Inc.
A MEMBER OF THE TAYLOR & FRANCIS GROUP
NEW YORK & LONDON / 1999

658.312404
K49t

Published in 1999 by
Garland Publishing Inc.
A Member of the Taylor & Francis Group
19 Union Square West
New York, NY 10003

10 9 8 7 6 5 4 3 2 1

Library of Congress Cataloging-in-Publication Data

Kim, Hyunjoo.
    Transcultural customization of international training programs / Hyunjoo
Kim.
        p. cm. — (Transnational business and corporate culture)
    Includes bibliographical references and index.
    ISBN 0-8153-3358-7 (alk. paper)
    1. Employees—Training of. 2. Intercultural communication. 3. Corpo-
rate culture. 4. International business enterprises—Employees—Training of.
I. Title. II. Series.
HF5549.5.T7K49 1999
658.3'12404—dc21   99-30366

Printed on acid-free, 250-year-life paper
Manufactured in the United States of America

Contents

Preface

The world is full of differences. People have different outlooks, speak different languages, eat different foods, wear different clothes, use different currencies, think differently, have different religions, value different things, behave differently, listen to different music, and have different social and political systems. One common thing is that the world is full of human being even though they are different. They just have different traditions and preferences.

In the emerging world in which we are living, we can easily find people who were born and grew up in a culture, have lived in other cultures, and have met and done business with people from different parts of the world. There is no clear cut right and wrong among cultural differences, and no one can experience all different cultures. People get to understand and value the differences. At the same time, however, a large number of our friends, family, and colleagues have not been exposed to cultures other than their own. What can we do to help them acknowledge the excitement of difference, understand others better, and benefit from the diverse experiences of others? What are the things we should keep to maintain our own identity? How can we help people to work together and cooperate with each other in different cultural contexts?

As we enter the twenty first century, the information and knowledge produced in the world has become enormous. How can we benefit from this? How can we overcome our differences and understand each other? How can we help others to understand the differences and think deeply and learn more from others without the fear of difference? What would be an effective and efficient way to obtain and convert others' accumulated experiences and intelligence to our own?

I tried to put together my professional experiences as an instructional designer and researcher with my personal exposure and reflections of different cultures. As an instructional designer working with customers from different cultural backgrounds, it has been a challenge to tailor my instruction to best serve their learning and facilitate the transfer of this learning to real life. It is a never-ending challenge to provide better solutions, which resolve clients' needs in a culturally adequate environment. As a researcher, I followed my intellectual curiosity and quest for best practices in the field of instructional systems design and management connected with these cultural issues. Now I want to share my research findings with other instructional designers and HR professionals so that they can be more flexible and effective as well as broaden their understanding of other cultures, and the process of transcultural customization.

It is the purpose of this book to provide a basic understanding of the changing world and different cultures, connect this understanding with the instructional design process in terms of cultural differences, and present a process for customizing training interventions transculturally.

The original case study for identifying a current status of transcultural customization process in action was possible in 1995 through the support of Motorola University who gave me an opportunity to look into their transcultural customization process. Although the organization itself has been changed in its structure and ways of providing training services to its various businesses within Motorola, Inc. and its customers, the case study will give readers a chance to understand what kinds of challenges an organization has in terms of providing and managing transcultural training interventions. A number of Motorola managers and instructional designers provided me their invaluable professional experiences and insights. I deeply appreciate their help.

PART I

A Context: Culture and Instructional Systems Design

CHAPTER 1

Where We Are in the Emerging World

As the world changes, the borders between countries have become more permeable. Many organizations in business and industry are targeting consumers both domestically and internationally (Marquardt & Reynolds, 1994). Companies have placed many of their manufacturing facilities, sales offices, partners, and/or suppliers outside of their home countries. Mergers and acquisitions have been undertaken without a sense of border to make more profitable organizations. Overseas investment has been one of the core business competencies aimed toward making more profits. Joint-ventures among culturally different organizations are appeared. As a result of global business strategies and actions, global organizations often hire local people in different countries who have different nationalities, languages, customs, ethnicity, social systems, and cultural traits. It is almost needless to say that the organizations are being globalized. In fact, globalization, which "represents the converging of economic and social forces generated by an increased sharing of social and economic values and opportunities" (Marquardt & Reynolds, 1994, p. 4), is crucial to organizational survival and growth in the 21st century. Globalization has begun before entering the new millennium.

With all kinds of management and strategic issues caused by the globalization of organizations, the training and education of worldwide employees emerge as important issues. International corporations are faced with a new challenge: how to train and educate their employees who have different cultural backgrounds while maintaining core corporate values.

Early this decade, many futurists and economists characterized the era we are living in as the *knowledge era* (Drucker, 1994; Marquardt & Reynolds, 1994). Knowledge provides the key raw material for the creation of wealth. It is a fountain of organizational and personal power. Due to the rapid development of new technology, manual labor-intensive work is becoming less important. Most organizations require people who have the knowledge and skills to perform their work, and who are able to manage the process of work to solve various kinds of problems and to come up with new ideas. Employees are moving from needing repetitive skills to needing a knowledge of how to deal with surprises and exceptions, from depending on memory and facts to being spontaneous and creative, from avoiding risks to taking risks, and from focusing on policies and procedures to building collaboration with people (Marquardt & Reynolds, 1994). The world economy now asks people to be ready for 'global standards.' No matter how experts in different fields define the global standards, it is true that the value of work and the meaning of employment have been changed. More importantly, human resources are the most valuable asset for organizations in the global economy of a knowledge society. Successful organizations in the knowledge era are learning organizations, in which every employee learns continuously and adds value to the organization. Thus, the learning organization should be able to manage its intellectual human resources and promote a learning culture. The learning culture should emphasize continuous learning and the appropriate transfer of learning to the work setting. The role of training and education in organizations is more critical than ever and should be stressed for the creation and maintenance of learning organizations in the global knowledge age.

BASIC STRATEGIES TO ORGANIZE LEARNING INTERVENTIONS

Over the past decades, many organizations have invested heavily in training and educating their employees (Lynton & Pareek, 1990). In 1992, according to the American Society for Training and Development, American corporations had already spent over 210 billion dollars on both formal and informal training activities (cited in King, 1994). The main purpose of training is to prepare employees to adequately perform their jobs (Treffman, 1978; Lynton & Pareek,

1990), to help employees to be effective problem solvers and lifelong learners, and eventually to maintain and increase the corporation's market share through the optimum performance of its employees. In the case of global organizations which have to deal with various cultures throughout the world, it is important to consider cultural differences in training and education systems. Each global organization may have different strategies to meet the needs of cultural adjustment based on its own business situation and goals. There are, however, basically four options for education and training systems:

(1) maintain a separate system in each country to design, develop and implement localized training programs;

(2) centralize systems for designing and developing training programs in a home country where the corporate headquarters are located, and transfer and implement the training programs to the offices in other cultures;

(3) combine (1) and (2); and

(4) outsource the training and education services.

If an organization can afford the necessary human resources, time, and money for designing, developing, and implementing training programs in each country separately, option (1) would be a good choice because each training program could be designed, developed and implemented to meet the local needs and the characteristics of the local employees. However, in many cases, it is difficult to provide adequate human resources, time, and monetary investment for each country in an organization. Even if sufficient resources are available, there might be many overlaps among the training programs which have basically the same goals and objectives across different countries in the organization. Much waste of resources could be avoided by transferring well-designed training programs between countries. Additionally, the goal of many organizations is to build one corporate culture throughout its worldwide offices. This leads to option (2), which is the centralization of the design and development function.

In option (2), training programs are transferred from one culture to the other. Any culture-specific components appearing in the training programs should be modified to fit into the local culture (Abbott, 1988). Unless the cultural differences are recognized and adapted to the local culture, the target audience could not be expected to learn optimally from the instruction (McAlpine, 1992). There are several prerequisites to making option (2) an effective strategy: (a) centralized design teams must have adequate human resources who know and reflect the local culture into the design and development of instruction, (b) the social and technological infrastructure of the local country must be developed to the point that it can support the development of training programs, and (c) local offices must have adequate human resources and budgets to support design and development activities associated with transfer and implementation.

However, issues related to cross-cultural differences are magnified in option (2). First, because the training programs are transferred to various cultures, depending on the target audience covered by each training course, it is required for the centralized training department to design and develop training programs with more sensitive awareness of cultural matters which might become an issue in various aspects of the instruction. These cultural issues might arise in the content of the materials, instructional activities, grouping of participants for activities, material development, delivery of instruction, etc. Second, even if there are identified needs which can be solved through a training program, the design and development of new training programs may be difficult at the local level due to the insufficient or limited instructional design capacity of local offices. Third, there is a possibility that the transferred training programs will not be effective because of cultural differences retained in the original course.

The best solution for the global organizations, if they have appropriate resources in their local training departments, is option (3) which combines the best of options (1) and (2). In option (3), centrally developed training programs are transferred from the main training department to local offices in different cultures and adapted for the local culture. Additionally, each local office maintains the potential to independently design and develop their own training programs to suit local needs. Thus, in option (3) the local offices can provide both transferred and originally developed training programs to the local audience.

Option (3) can be implemented by providing systematic tools and guidance, and by institutionalizing a systematic instructional design approach in the local offices of the organization. Therefore, the customization specialists can conduct transcultural customization projects adequately to deliver effective and efficient training programs to the local employees. In addition, they can design and develop any necessary training programs systematically as the systematic approach is locally institutionalized.

When an overseas office is in a start-up stage, an option (4) might be an effective solution. After locating a high-quality training and education services institution, the local office can purchase pre-packaged training programs as needed. In this case, careful review of the program and the customization of it to meet the organization's needs is critical. The program provider must understand the culture of the organization and be able to incorporate the customers' specific needs and organizational culture.

NEEDS FOR ISD APPROACH TO TRANSCULTURAL CUSTOMIZATION

The concepts of instructional systems design (ISD) for the development of effective and efficient training programs have been institutionalized by many businesses and industries. Over a decade ago, the Rand Corporation and the Human Resources Organization exemplified attempts to apply the systems approach to the design of training (Reiser, 1987). ISD and its related disciplines, such as performance technology, have been used for diagnosing performance problems, providing solutions for the problems, designing and developing instructional intervention which has been justified by preliminary analyses, and for implementing and evaluating the solutions for resolving problems in organizations. There are many ISD models which describe the process or procedures for designing and developing effective and efficient instructions which are used in various educational learning environments (Andrews & Goodson, 1991; Gustafson & Tillman, 1991; Gustafson & Powell, 1991). According to Andrews and Goodson (1991), instructional design models serve four purposes: (a) improvement of learning and instruction by the use of a systematic approach, (b) improvement of management of instructional design and development, (c) improvement of the evaluation process, and (d) testing or building of learning theory.

Many organizations have developed their own ISD models to design and develop instruction to better fit their own working environment and organizational culture. However, specialized ISD models assume that the models would be used in one culture, such as in the previously described option (1) case. According to Hites (1991), "while various techniques or methods exist, there are no complete, integrated models for the design and delivery of instruction across cultures" (p. 9). There is ample evidence that people learn better when the instruction is relevant to their own experience and culture (Keller, 1987a, b; Morical & Tsai, 1992). Instructional designers should make sure that the training programs are culturally relevant to their target audience, because a training program which is developed in one culture does not always work the same way in another culture (Abbott, 1988; Morical & Tsai, 1992).

NEEDS FOR A TRANSCULTURAL CUSTOMIZATION PROCESS

Not many research studies have been done regarding the issue of transcultural transfer of instructional interventions in the field of instructional systems. The term 'transcultural' has a similar meaning to 'cross-cultural.' However, in this book, transcultural is used specifically for a transfer of a product, which is designed and developed for a specific culture rather than cross-culture, from one culture to another. Cross-cultural refers to the intellectual process by which two or more cultural groups are compared (Motorola, 1993) as well as an incorporation of information and values of a second culture on an equal basis with the original culture (Marquardt & Reynolds, 1994). In fact, a product or instruction which is designed and developed cross-culturally is easier to customize transculturally for the recipient cultures. Another similar term is 'multicultural.' Multicultural refers to a structure of gathering diverse cultures in a setting or in a group (Motorola, 1993).

Most research of cultural differences has been conducted primarily in the fields of anthropology, sociology, business, communication, or international/cross-cultural/multicultural education. While those fields focus primarily on cultural differences to resolve academic and/or practical questions, the issues of effective and efficient learning across borders and cultures should be studied in the field of ISD to resolve new questions raised in the global learning environment of the knowledge era.

In this book, 'transcultural customization' refers to an adaptation or modification of something being transferred from one culture to another to fit better into the local culture of the recipients. Thus, transcultural customization of training programs is an adaptation or modification of any instructional system and/or intervention, which is developed in one culture, for implementation in another culture.

Historically, transcultural customization has been limited to literal translation of training programs. Real customization usually happens during the class by instructors who deliver the instruction. In these cases, the nature of instruction is not much different from that of instruction done by a traditional approach which mostly depends on subject matter experts to design and deliver the instruction. Even if the original instruction was designed and developed systematically using the ISD approach and the effectiveness and efficiency of the instruction was proved, one cannot assume that the same instruction would work exactly the same way in a different cultural context. People in different cultures have their own unique needs, learning styles, learning environment, and/or instructional hardware and software available. Thus, it is presumed that the quality, effectiveness and efficiency of instruction transferred to a new cultural context may be diminished if the customization of instruction is not systematically conducted.

The primary purpose of this book is to present a systematic model for transcultural customization of training programs in global organizations. The transfer of instruction across cultures will be studied from the perspective of a systems approach to propose a procedural model for transcultural customization of training programs. A case study of Motorola, Inc. has been conducted to identify current processes, systems, and problems of the transcultural customization practices in a global organization.

Although a procedural model would not be the only solution to the previously stated problem, it provides a systematic approach to finding the optimum solution to the problem. There are already numerous models of instructional design for different settings. According to Gustafson and Tillman (1991), the principle differences of currently available models of instructional design involve:

(1) where the model is to be applied (e.g., military, business, higher education, or public school);

(2) whether the outcome is expected to be a product for distribution and used by people other than its designers;

(3) whether design and development is to be an individual or a team effort; and

(4) whether the emphasis is primarily on designing new materials or selecting from among those that already exist. (p. 9)

These areas of differences, however, could be interpreted as indicating the need for a new model. In other words, a new model may be necessary if there are distinct needs in those four areas which cannot be resolved by the current models. In fact, there are generally strong needs for a model for transcultural customization of training programs in the four following areas:

(1) global business organizations, which reflect recent trends and changes of the world, are the environments in which the model will be applied;

(2) the outcome of the model is expected to be transculturally customized training programs for distribution and used by the customization specialists who are responsible for the transcultural customization process;

(3) the design and development will be a team effort by a group of people who will play various roles in the customization process, including new roles and responsibilities such as customization specialists, translators, and cultural subject matter experts; and

(4) the emphasis of the model is on transferring existing training programs from one culture to another rather than on designing new instructional interventions or selecting training programs from among existing ones.

The model which will be presented in this book will have the descriptive, prescriptive, and predictive elements which Andrews and Goodson (1991) identify along with the explanatory element from their comparative analysis study of models of instructional design. The model will describe the systematic process of transcultural customization of training programs, with objectives to be achieved in each step throughout the process. At the same time, the model will prescribe:

(1) activities to be performed by the customization team;

(2) questions which a customization instructional designer, who is responsible for the transcultural customization process, could ask himself or herself to accomplish the activities;

(3) roles or functions which should be played to complete each step;

(4) resources required; and

(5) products of each step.

The systematic nature of the model will ensure and predict the effectiveness and efficiency of the customized training programs. Additionally, the model with the above features will facilitate the performance of novice customization specialists as they conduct transcultural customization projects.

CHAPTER 2

What the Past Teaches Us

The transcultural customization process should be understood from a
cultural perspective and an instructional systems approach, in order to
have a deep understanding of culture which is implicitly imbedded in
the instruction and to utilize a systematic process for customization. We
can learn much from the vast body of research in the areas of culture
and instructional systems design. A review of culture theories will
guide an understanding of cultural differences and provide a basis of
transcultural transfer of instructional interventions in global
organizations. Also, the relationships between instructional systems
design and transcultural transfer and use of training processes and
products will be discussed to link instructional systems design (ISD)
with transcultural issues and to learn from the available research studies
and practices in the field.

THEORIES OF CULTURE

Bhola (1990) defines culture as "all that is imagined, expressed,
thought, patterned, instituted, woven, fabricated, dug, dammed and
built by human beings" (p. 4). Whereas Hofstede (1993) defines culture
as "the collective programming of the mind which distinguishes one
group or category of people from another" (p. 89). Culture is made by
human beings through the influence of a group's religion, language,
geographical closeness, educational systems, type of government, the
society's class structure, and the rate of technological change (Gannon,
1994).

Although every culture is distinct from one another, some cultures
share more similar things than others. Some cultural researchers (e.g.,

Hall & Hall, 1990; Hofstede, 1980, 1993; O'Hara-Devereaux & Johansen, 1994; Trompenaars, 1993) identify cultures along certain dimensions, based on their research, observations and live interactions with various cultures. When cultures are described using the framework of dimensions of culture, which could be defined as comparative categorizations of culture, there is no definite position for each culture. Rather cultures are scattered along a line in-between the extremes in various dimensions.

Although there are some differences in the specific dimensions of culture identified by different researchers, most categorizations are found to overlap. Commonly agreed upon cultural dimensions in literature are

Individualism versus Collectivism

This dimension focuses on people's orientation of attitude. *Individualism* is described as a prime orientation to the self (Trompenaars, 1993). They use "I" frequently when speaking, prefer to take individual responsibility and to achieve tasks alone (Trompenaars, 1993), and take care of themselves and of their immediate families only (Hofstede, 1980).

In collectivistic culture, people tend to be group-oriented (Trompenaars, 1993). *Collectivism* is described as a prime orientation to common goals and objectives (Trompenaars, 1993) and "is characterized by a tight social framework in which people distinguish between in-groups and out-groups" (Hofstede, 1980, p. 45). They use "we" frequently when speaking. They prefer to cluster and take group responsibility.

Context: Specific versus Diffuse

The dimension of context focuses on how deeply people get involved with other people. In *specific* culture, also known as *low context* culture (Hall & Hall, 1990; O'Hara-Devereaux & Johansen, 1994), people allow other people only into specific areas of life, for instance only in the work place for a business relationship or only in a club for a social relationship. They tend to split work and private life and to have high mobility. People are consistent in their dialogue within these areas regardless of to whom and where they speak (Hall & Hall, 1990; Trompenaars, 1993).

In *diffuse* culture, which is also called as *high context* culture (Hall & Hall, 1990; O'Hara-Devereaux & Johansen, 1994), people tend to consider that work and private life are closely linked. They are consistent in their approach to something or someone; for instance, "Herr Doktor Muller is Herr Doktor Muller at his university, at the butcher's and the garage" (Trompenaars, 1993, p. 75). They will, however, say different things to different people.

Time: Sequential versus Synchronic and Short-term versus Long-term

In *sequential time-oriented* culture (Trompenaars, 1993), which is the same as *monochronic* culture (Hall & Hall, 1990; O'Hara-Devereaux & Johansen, 1994), people only do one activity at a time. Time is measurable to them. They tend to concentrate on the job to be done and to hold strictly to appointments. They emphasize precision and are used to superficial, short-term relationships. They much prefer to follow plans and tasks (Hall & Hall, 1990; Trompenaars, 1993).

In *synchronic time-oriented* culture (Trompenaars, 1993), which is *polychronic* culture (Hall & Hall, 1990; O'Hara-Devereaux & Johansen, 1994), people do more than one activity at one time. Time is elastic and flexible to them. They are easily distracted and consider appointment, agenda, or deadlines as desirable, but not as ends in themselves. Establishing social relationships is a priority to them. Also, developing lifetime relationships is more important than a meeting's content objectives. They can easily change details or plans (Hall & Hall, 1990; Trompenaars, 1993).

There is another time related dimension: *short-term* versus *long-term* orientation (Hall & Hall, 1993; Hofstede, 1993; Trompenaars, 1993). *Short-term oriented* culture values the past and present, such as respect for tradition and fulfilling social obligations. Conversely *long-term oriented* culture values the future.

Other Cultural Dimensions

In addition to those dimensions of culture, Trompenaars (1993) categorized four more dimensions to understand different cultures:

(1) *universalism* versus *particularism* which have different points of moral reference. *Universalistic* people tends to behave based on the social and legal norms, while *particularistic* people tend to follow personal relationships;

(2) *neutral* versus *affective* which represent the degree of expression of emotions. *Affective* people expresses his/her emotions more immediately than *neutral* people;

(3) *achievement* versus *ascription* which characterize the origin of status whether the status is from the background of a person or the ability of a person. *Achievement-oriented* culture does not value and use formal titles as much as *ascription-oriented* culture in which people unconditionally respect the power of hierarchical superiors and seniors. Instead, *achievement-oriented* culture uses titles related to competencies and values of personal ability; and

(4) *internal* versus *external* control which indicates the location of control between environment and oneself. People in *internal control* culture think they, as individuals, are in control rather than that the environment controls or influences their actions or decisions which is more *external control* culture. Consequently, internal control people tend to be more self oriented than external control people who tend to seek group harmony and are willing to compromise and adapt to the environment.

Hofstede (1980) has also conducted extensive research on national cultures in 40 countries over a period of six years and categorized culture into four dimensions. His dimensions include *individualism* versus *collectivism*, which was explained previously, along with three other dimensions:

(1) *power distance* which "indicates the extent to which a society accepts the fact that power in institutions and organizations is distributed unequally" (p. 45). In a *small power distance* culture, hierarchy means an inequality of roles, established for convenience. Thus superiors and subordinates consider each other to be the same kind of people, whereas people in a similar hierarchy from a *large power distance* culture are considered to

be different kinds of people since the hierarchy means existential inequality;

(2) *uncertainty avoidance* which indicates the degree of tolerance a society has towards uncertainty and ambiguity. *Strong uncertainty avoidance* culture seeks absolute truths and values, needs written rules and regulations to be kept rigidly, and is concerned with security in life, while *weak uncertainty avoidance* culture focuses on relativism and empiricism, sets minimal rules, and is more willing to take risks in life; and

(3) *masculinity* versus *femininity* by which a society's values are dominated. In a *masculine* culture, sex roles are clearly differentiated so as that men should be assertive and women should be nurturing. Also, performance, work, money, and things are important. In *feminine* culture, sex roles are more fluid, and quality of life, people and environment are of value.

Whereas Hofstede and Trompenaars focus on cultural differences from the perspective of management, Hall and Hall (1990) have a communications perspective. Hall and Hall (1990) explain cultural differences regarding space, fast and slow messages, releasing the right responses, action chains, and interfacing, to provide key concepts of underlying structures of culture. The categories by Hall and Hall (1990) also include high and low context, monochronic and polychronic time, past- and future-oriented culture, and information flow. In fact, Hall and Hall's study relates in large part to O'Hara-Devereaux & Johansen's five cultural lenses.

O'Hara-Devereaux and Johansen (1994) visualize different dimensions in a graphical form as shown in Figure 1. They categorize culture into five dimensions, which they call "five cultural lenses" including the common categories explained above such as high and low *contexts* and monochronic and polychronic *time*.

The other three dimensions are:

(1) *language* as a means to the written or oral communication. Although language is not considered a dimension of culture, it is still an important factor in shaping cultural differences;

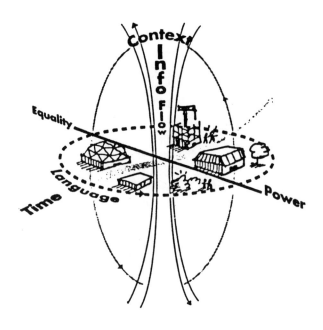

Figure 1. The five cultural variables in holographic relationship

Note: From M. O'Hara-Devereaux & R. Johansen, 1994, Globalwork:
    Bridging distance, culture, and time, p. 51. Copyright 1994 by
    Jossey-Bass Publishers, San Francisco.

(2) degree of *equality/power* which represent "the distance and types of relationships between people and groups" (p. 50). This dimension is similar to power distance as explained by Hofstede (1980); and

(3) *information flow* between people and levels in organization as well as the action chains moving toward communication or task completion, consisting of the path and the speed of communication.

Table 1 summarizes the cultural dimensions discussed by several researchers in theories of culture. The check marks indicate dimensions categorized and explained by different researchers.

It is the purpose of a review of theories of culture to provide a framework for understanding cultures and cultural differences, rather than to define a specific culture and to find out how a culture changes in the context of anthropological and sociological interests. Although the researchers have not exhaustively tested every single culture around the world to come up with the dimensions of culture, their idea of cultural dimensions provide a basic framework for understanding cultures and cultural differences. In addition, it is important to acknowledge that every culture has different meaning system, values, attitudes and behavioral patterns in order to understand others in different culture and to utilize the understanding of cultural differences in providing culturally acceptable instructions.

The dimensions of culture can help instructional designers and customization specialists to understand cultural differences in various dimensions, to determine how to design instruction based on the culture of the target audience, to find out why some things work in one culture but not in another, and to identify what should be customized depending on the target audience's cultural background.

INSTRUCTIONAL SYSTEMS DESIGN AND CULTURE

People perceive, think, and learn differently depending on their cultural background. Considering global organizations which have employees and clients with diverse cultural backgrounds, there are many opportunities to design and deliver training programs for employees and clients internationally. In fact, it is a challenge for instructional designers to design and adapt training to meet the needs of culturally

Table 1: Cultural Dimensions Discussed by Various Researchers

Dimensions of Culture	Hall & Hall (1990)	Hofstede (1980)	O'Hara-Devereaux & Johansen (1994)	Trompenaars (1993)
Individualism & Collectivism		X		X
Low & High Context	X		X	X
Time (Monochronic & Polychronic; Past- & Future-Oriented)	X		X	X
Emotions (Neutral & effective)			X	X
Ascription & Achievement-Oriented				X
Internal & External Control				X
Weak (Particularism) & Strong (Universalism) Uncertainty avoidance		X		X
Space (Territoriality; Personal space)	X		X	
Information flow (Path & Speed of Communications)	X		X	
Small & Large Power Distance		X	X	
Masculinity & Femininity		X		

adiverse audiences (Morical & Tsai, 1992).

ISD Defined

The concepts and applications of instructional systems design have been in place in various instructional and educational settings for about forty years. The definition of ISD can be synthesized as a systematic process of designing, developing, implementing, and evaluating the total process and complete systems of learning and teaching (AECT, 1977; Reiser, 1987; Richey, 1986) although the actual terms defined in literature also include: instructional design, instructional development, systems approach, instructional technology, and educational technology. The term ISD has been referred to and used interchangeably with those terms (Gustafson & Powell, 1991; Gustafson & Tillman, 1991; Reiser, 1987).

Rothwell and Kazanas (1992) describe the characteristics of ISD, from the perspective of human performance in organizations, as: "(1) an emerging profession, (2) focused on establishing and maintaining efficient and effective human performance, (3) guided by a model of human performance, (4) carried out systematically, (5) based on open systems theory, and (6) oriented to finding and applying the most cost-effective solutions to human performance problems" (p. 3). With those characteristics, ISD is differentiated from the traditional approach to the development of instruction. King (1994) summarizes the features of the traditional and systems approaches to development of instruction into six categories (see Table 2).

Although the basic principles of ISD potentially work in any culture, how to implement the principles may differ from one culture to another. For instance, while reinforcement will always improve the quality and increase the quantity of performance being reinforced when it is used appropriately, positive reinforcement in one culture may be a punisher, or a negative, in another culture (Thiagarajan, 1988). Some details of instruction, such as culturally specific content, specific reinforcer, instructional strategy, instructional delivery method, etc., should be carefully customized when instructional interventions are traveling across borders (Abbott, 1988). Thus, it is important to understand the culture of each target population, which affects learning, and cultural differences between different target population groups.

Table 2: Features of the Traditional and Systems Approaches to the Development of Instructional Programs

Features	Traditional Approach	Systems Approach
Underlying theory	Developmental theory	General systems theory
Role of participants		
Subject matter expert	Originator/developer of instructional materials	Provider of content information from which instruction is developed
Teacher/instructor	Primary source of instructional information Deliverer of instruction	Facilitator of instructional process Guide to instructional material
Participant	Recipient of SME-developed and teacher-delivered lessons	Participant in the development and use of instructional material
Designer	None	Developer/evaluator of instructional content, instructional activities and assessment strategies
Derivation of content	Subject matter expert opinion	Needs, job, task analysis Analysis of instructional goal
Derivation of information for revisions	Subject matter expert opinion Teacher opinion	Participant performance and attitude data Expert review
Focus of educational process	Teaching	Learning
Measures of achievement	Norm-referenced assessment	Criterion-referenced assessment

Note: From D. S, King, 1994, Development of a formative evaluation model for instructor-led courses, p. 2.

ISD Models

One characteristic of ISD could be identified as the utilization of a systematic process in the design of instruction. This characteristic appears in many existing ISD models for designing instruction (e.g., Dick & Carey, 1990; Hannum & Hansen, 1992; Mager, 1988; Romiszowski, 1981; Rothwell & Kazanas, 1992). ISD models are used as: (a) communication devices among people involved in instructional development, (b) instructional development project management guides, and/or (c) prescriptive decision making tools (Gustafson & Powell, 1991). King (1994) specifically points out that the procedural models allow practitioners to apply and use instructional theory.

Gustafson and Powell (1991) have reviewed some of the ISD models, classified them into three categories of a taxonomy, and described their trends. According to Gustafson and Powell (1991), "the taxonomy provides a vehicle for examining the assumptions and conditions associated with any [ISD] model and places it in a scheme for easy understanding" (p. 15). The three categories divided by the taxonomy are: (a) classroom focus, (b) product focus, and (c) systems focus (Gustafson & Powell, 1991).

Some of the assumptions that the currently available ISD models have could be presumed from Gustafson and Powell's analysis of models: (a) the ISD models are for designing, developing and implementing new instruction rather than a modification or customization of existing instruction, and (b) the outputs of the ISD process that the models propose to go through are produced for a homogeneous culture, because the models do not offer considerations specifically to understand different cultures. Hites (1991) also points out the lack of complete, integrated ISD models which provide any considerations of cultural difference for the design and delivery of instruction across cultures.

Use of Technology

Another characteristic of ISD would be the use of appropriate technology for enhancing the learning process, ranging from the use of simple graphics to the use of computers, multimedia, and telecommunication devices such as satellites and networks. There are cultural differences in perceptions of technology, names and uses of technology, and in the level of technological advancement in daily life and in the learning process and environment. Pettersson (1982) has studied cultural differences in the perception of image and color in pictures and found that different cultures have difference preferences for color use, possibly due to each group's ability to see or experience various colors in their natural environment. Thus, depending on the target audience, use of color and detail should be designed and developed differently.

For more complicated technology, such as computers, to be used and transferred in different cultures, Reynolds (1990) suggests general and technical considerations for producing successful automated training programs across cultures: (a) keep the lessons simple, (b) ensure clarity of explanation in content, (c) anticipate foreign use and different display format, (d) consider text characteristics caused by different language system, and (e) be prepare for software snags. Trollip and Brown (1987) also insist the importance of consideration for the possibility of different language versions of software for relatively easy implementation. However, as Collis and De Diana (cited in Ely, 1990) point out, the human side of educational software portability is more difficult to solve than that of the technical side. This point stresses the importance of cultural adjustment.

TRANSCULTURAL TRANSFER AND USE OF TRAINING PROCESSES AND PRODUCTS

Transcultural transfer of training processes and products occurs when existing training processes and products which were designed and developed in one culture are delivered and implemented in other cultures. Transcultural transfer requires an appropriate cultural customization or adaptation process for successful learning by participants in the training programs. Morical and Tsai (1992) describe the meaning of cultural adaptation as:

> ... [P]resenting the basic principle, theory, or concept of a training program in such a way that people in another culture can understand and apply it. The core content remains unchanged. But the way in which it is discussed, presented, and explained is tailored to local users. (p. 65)

Ely (1983, 1989a, 1989b, 1990) has done comprehensive research on the diffusion of educational technology and cross-cultural transfer of instructional technology and materials. He points out the importance of transcultural customization, although he uses the term 'cultural translation' which "has to follow a systematic process of analysis, review, and evaluation by representatives of ultimate audience" (Ely, 1983, p. 14). Further, Ely (1983, 1990) provides guidelines for cultural translation of instructional materials, especially for cross-cultural software portability. Here, 'portability' can be understood as easy transferability. The guidelines consider linguistic factors, instructional factors, structural factors, motivational factors, content verification, learner verification, revision, and group testing as presented in Table 3 (Ely, 1990). The major points of Ely's guidelines are consideration of the translation process, cultural adaptation of the content area, instructional strategy, and formative evaluation with representatives of the target population for cross-cultural transfer of instruction.

Although Ely (1990) has developed these guidelines specifically for software portability, he addresses the important issues around the cross-cultural transfer of instructional materials: appropriateness and time/cost.

These two issues are directly related to learning effectiveness and efficiency, which are fundamental goals of ISD (Rothwell & Kazanas, 1992). Also, many factors in the guidelines are applicable for transcultural customization such as translation considerations, use of local examples and analogies, and formative evaluation with local learners. In addition, the guidelines emphasize that the principles of ISD and related theories are not changed cross-culturally, as pointed out previously: structural, motivational and revision factors in the guidelines are important principles for utilizing ISD to design and develop any new instructional interventions (see Table 3 for detailed factors in the guidelines).

It is arguable, however, that the factors in the guidelines are not sufficient and could be modified for the transcultural customization process, because the guidelines are developed for cross-cultural transfer of software. First of all, front-end analysis may be necessary for transcultural customization. For instance, it is essential to analyze: (a) the local target audience's characteristics as learners, (b) the cultural context of the learning environment including both the physical and the

Table 3: Guidelines for Cross-Cultural Software Portability

	Check one in each column					
	Column 1 Need			Column 2 Value		
1.0 Linguistic factors						
1.1 Arrange for translation by person familiar with relevant local education settings						
1.2 Translate into the most common dialect						
1.3 Simplify the language						
2.0 Instructional factors						
2.1 Delete irrelevant content						
2.2 Add examples and analogies of local people and activities						
2.3 Break work into small units						
2.4 Lengthen instructional time (if applicable)						
3.0 Structural factors						
3.1 Add an advance organizer						
3.2 Increase learner participation						
3.2.1 Require frequent overt responses						
3.2.2 Permit group and individual participation						
3.3 Provide feedback and transfer exercises						
3.4 Establish (final) closure						
4.0 Motivational factors						
4.1 Attract attention at the beginning						
4.2 Relate content to personal and local interests						
4.3 Bring out the immediate an longer term relevance						
4.4 Help learners to gain confidence in responses						
4.5 Allow learners to express satisfaction						
5.0 Content verification						
5.1 Subject matter specialist reviews software with regard to :						
5.1.1 Accuracy						
5.1.2 Thoroughness						
5.1.3 Conceptual validity						

Table 3 (continued)

	Check one in each column			
	Column 1 Need		Column 2 Value	
6.0 Learner verification				
6.1 Tryout with 4-6 representative learners				
6.2 Approximate actual conditions of use				
6.3 Ask learner to "think aloud" about what he/she is doing; ask question about confusing parts				
6.4 Debrief learner about matters of:				
6.4.1 Difficulty				
6.4.2 Pacing/length				
6.4.3 Language				
6.4.4 Examples and analogies				
6.4.5 Activities				
6.4.6 Engagement and relevance				
6.4.7 Satisfaction				
6.5 Discuss results of debriefing with teacher-users				
7.0 Revision				
7.1 Revise using data from 6.4 above				
7.2 Use guidelines from sections 1.0 through 5.0				
7.3 Plan for implementation in teaching/learning setting				
8.0 Group testing				
8.1 Prepare criterion test				
8.2 Check prerequisite knowledge and skills of learners				
8.3 Distribute material to be learned				
8.4 Administer criterion test upon completion of learning task				
8.5 Analyze test results				
8.6 Revise as necessary				
8.7 Repeat steps 8.2 through 8.6 with new subjects				

Note: From "Portability: Cross-cultural educational perspectives," by D. P. Ely, 1990, *Journal of Research on Computing in Education, 23*, pp. 276-277.

Table 4: Recommendations for Design and Delivery of Cross-Cultural Training

Method or Design Activities	Recommendations
Front-end analysis or formative evaluation	• Include international members on design team
	• Make fewer assumptions about audience
	• Analyze language competency, value differences, expectations, cultural adjustment problems and motivation,.
	• Conduct by mail or train in-country personnel to conduct front-end analysis
	• Provide adequate lead time and resources for front-end analysis
	• Adequate front-end analysis insures appropriate objectives
Instructional strategies	
Activating motivation	Little apparent difference
Informing of objectives	
Directing attention	
Recalling prerequisites	
Stimulus presentation (verbal or written)	• Use simple language
	• Slow pace of delivery
	• Provide glossaries of terms/acronyms
	• Avoid idioms, jargon
	• Write unfamiliar terms on board
	• Encourage questions
Stimulus presentation (visual)	• Use visuals liberally
	• Use models and demonstrations
Learning guidance	• Make examples specific, relevant
	• Use metric units

Table 4 (continued)

Method or Design Activities	Recommendations
Enhancing retention	• Reiterate concepts several ways
	• Review, summarize frequently
	• Translate summaries
Practice	• Practice frequently
	• Practice small chunks
Eliciting performance	• Check comprehension frequently, through observation and written exercises
	• Ask participants to explain, or demonstrate what they have learned
Providing feedback	• Avoid direct pressure
	• Avoid negative feedback to an individual in front of the group
Management strategies	• Use interpreters
	• Translate participant materials
	• Give frequent breaks for reading, rest, questions, translation
	• Attend to "housekeeping" needs
Delivery strategies	• Avoid rushing
	• Avoid crowding
	• Use media with multiple channels
	• Use self-paced media (with instructors to answer questions)
Evaluation	• Gain participants' trust
	• Observe performance over extended period
	• Use a variety of evaluation methods: quizzes, observation, listening to participant comments

Note: From J. M. Hites, 1991, The design and delivery of training for international students: A case study, pp. 6-8.

affective environment, and (c) the availability and compatibility of local delivery systems including both hardware and software.

Another interesting research study in cross-cultural training has been conducted by Hites (1991). This research is based on a case study of a global organization in business and industry. Although this research is also focused on the design and delivery of new courses for a cross-cultural audience, rather than on the transcultural customization of existing courses, the list of recommendations in five design activities for cross-cultural target audience has many useful suggestions for transcultural customization. The recommendations are made around: (a) front-end analysis which is not covered in Ely's guidelines, (b) instructional strategies integrating Gagné's nine events of instruction, (c) management strategies for accommodating participants' language differences and cultural needs, (d) delivery strategies, and (e) evaluation of participants' performance (Hites, 1991). The specific recommendations are presented in Table 4.

Although both Ely (1990) and Hites (1991) suggest important considerations for cross-cultural design and delivery of instructional interventions, they do not provide a systematic process for cross-cultural ISD activities. Thus, Ely's guidelines and Hites' recommendations have beneficial implications but may not provide sufficient guidelines for the transcultural customization of training programs. In addition, because the guidelines and recommendations have been developed around cross-cultural design and transfer of instruction, the focus is somewhat different from the transcultural customization of instruction. For instance, Ely (1990) and Hites (1991) suggest including local and international members on design teams for the cross-cultural portability process. The local designer, however, should have a key role in the process of transcultural customization. Consequently, the perspective of looking at the transcultural customization process should be shifted from the original designer's cultural point of view, which is cross-cultural, to the local designer's cultural point of view, which is transcultural.

Summary

Not many research studies have been done focusing on the transcultural customization of training processes and products in the field of ISD. There is not much evidence concerning how global organizations practice transcultural customization. In a global knowledge era, it is expected that a systematic process of transcultural customization of training processes and products would help to reduce design cycle time, to ensure quality, to enhance learning across diverse target audiences, and further to facilitate the development of a global learning organization.

Finally, Bennett (1986) states

> Cultural difference is neither good nor bad, it is just different. One's own culture is not any more central to reality than any other culture, although it may be preferable to a particular individual or group. (p. 46)

As individuals with specific cultural backgrounds, instructional designers or transcultural customization specialists should be aware of and appreciate cultural differences to design and develop instruction cross-culturally and/or to customize training programs transculturally.

IMPLICATIONS FROM THE EARLIER STUDIES

A Systematic Process of Transcultural Customization

Even if a course is originally designed and developed using the systems approach, one cannot guarantee that the course will be effective in a new environment with a culturally different target audience. The customization process should be performed using the systems approach. The course itself should be reviewed systematically. The local target audience of the course should be analyzed. The course materials should be developed and produced locally based on the customization results. Therefore, a systematic process of transcultural customization should follow the five main phases which most ISD models are based on: analysis, design, development, evaluation, and implementation.

Understanding of Culture as a Competency for Customization Specialists

The transcultural customization process involves at least two different cultures: one is a culture of the original course; and the other is a culture where the original course is brought in and modified locally. The customization specialists should be aware of the cultural differences and be able to apply their understanding of culture in the process.

The understanding of cultural differences is an important skill for customization specialists who are responsible for the transcultural customization process. The customization specialist is responsible for the entire customization process of training programs. He/she manages the whole customization process, organizes teams as the phases evolve, conducts actual activities, and monitors team members' activities and the quality of their performance.

Additionally, the understanding of different cultures is an important skill for instructional designers who design and develop original courses which have global target audiences. The instructional designers should be able to provide various examples, alternative instructional strategies, and an instructional delivery system for culturally diverse target populations. Thus, target audience analysis should be designed and performed carefully for the global population in cooperation with regional offices. Some important tasks are the identification of language requirements, and the identification and consideration of various local infrastructure which support the local organizational environment and society in general. They also must be careful to use the appropriate level of language to be globally understood.

Involvement of Cultural Subject Matter Experts (CSMEs) in the Customization Process

Depending on the difficulty of the cultural nature of the original course, CSMEs provide culturally specific knowledge of the history, culture, society, environment, politics, economics and business of a local organization. Their input would be useful to customize courses that fit culturally into the local environment. Some CSME candidates are local SMEs, local employees, customization specialists, and cultural specialists, such as historians and cross-cultural training specialists. It is preferable to have CSMEs who have experiences in different cultures so that they can distinguish the local culture from other cultures.

Involvement of Local Subject Matter Experts in the Customization Process

Subject matter experts (SMEs) provide knowledge, skills and/or attitude-related expertise for creating and customizing courses. They could be located centrally in business headquarters and/or locally in a local region. It is important to obtain local SMEs' input for the customization process. Local SMEs would be more familiar with the local target audience than central SMEs. As SMEs, they must have a level of expertise on the subject similar to those who are involved in designing the original course. Local SMEs might play a role as technical developers by writing necessary content, or assisting technical developers by providing necessary knowledge and information.

Modification of Content Based on the Local Culture

By using dimensions of culture, examples, instructional strategies, learning activities and instructional delivery methods could be analyzed and modified to adapt to the local culture. For instance, an original course designed in the US may have many class discussions among peers as a learning activity. In terms of information flow (O'Hara-Devereaux & Johansen, 1994), peer interaction and communication is well-accepted in the US. If the course is to be adapted for use in China, the course could be modified with less peer interaction and more instructor-led communication than the original course, since the role of a teacher is highly respected in Chinese culture. This is one of the findings from the case study of Motorola.

Other Implications

The following are other implications from the review of the literature:

1. modifications of instructional strategy, instructional delivery method, and learning environment based on the local culture;
2. consideration of the translation process;
3. formative evaluation with a local target audience;
4. emphasis of front-end analyses of needs assessment, cultural context analysis, and the local target audience analysis.

A Process for Transcultural Customization of Instructional Interventions

Part II is to explain and help in the utilization of the Transcultural Customization Model. The model was developed to guide instructional designers and/or customization specialists in global organizations who are responsible for customizing training courses to perform such projects in a systematic approach. Those who do not have an established process for customization will find the guidelines especially useful as they follow the explanations for the process for transcultural customization of training programs.

The model suggests an ideal process for customizing training programs. The model can be modified depending on the organizational situations, such as human resources, project budget, physical learning environment, instructional hardware and software availability, and so forth.

Definition of Customization

Customization is a systematic process of purposeful modification of any intervention in order to meet a specific organization's needs, goals, and cultural context. Customization includes analysis, design, development, evaluation and implementation of instructional design processes.

Assumptions for Customization

The Model for Transcultural Customization of Training Programs can be implemented in a global organization when the following assumptions are met:

- *Needs for a training program have been drawn from business or strategic planning, and/or reactive performance analyses;*

- *The solution, or a part of the solution, for resolving the identified needs is a training course;*

- *There is a training course available which meets the needs of the organization but has been developed in another culture; and*

- *The transcultural customization of a training program is conducted by a region which imported a training program developed in another region.*

If the above assumptions are not true, then a needs assessment should be conducted before transcultural customization of a training course is conducted, and/or a new training course should be designed and developed.

Structure of the Model Document

The guidelines for explaining and utilizing the Transcultural Customization Model are developed around a systematic process of customization. An overview of the entire process is shown on page 40.

The model is explained in the order of five basic phases of instructional design: Analysis, Customization Design, Development, Formative Evaluation, and Implementation. Each phase consists of several steps. In addition, each step consists of six elements which are indicated by the following icons:

 Objectives

What should be accomplished in the steps.

 Activities

What activities could be involved and performed to accomplish each step's objectives.

Questions

Questions asked in conducting activities or gathering information.

 Team

Who might be involved and/or what roles should be performed in accomplishing the objectives of the steps.

 Resources

Resources needed in accomplishing the objectives of the steps.

 Products

Final products resulting from the steps.

Team Members Referred to in the Guidelines

The Customization Team suggested in this document is for the optimal customization project.

Customization Specialist is responsible for the entire customization process of training courses as a customization project manager and instructional designer. Customization specialist conducts actual activities of a customization project and manages the whole customization process, such as organizing teams and monitoring team members' activities and qualities of their performances. Customization specialist is a native personnel in a region. It is beneficial if a customization specialist is also fluent in the language to communicate with people in the region where the original course was developed.

Original Instructional Designer (OID) is one originally responsible for designing, developing, evaluating and implementing the original course. The OID is in a region where the course was developed. The OID's cooperation is highly recommended for the whole process, especially for the analysis phase. If the OID is not available for consulting a customization project, you should utilize alternative methods such as attending a class and a train-the-trainer session of the original training program, analyzing instructional design documents and training materials, and interviewing instructors.

Subject Matter Experts (SMEs) provide knowledge, skills and/or attitude related expertise for customizing courses. They could be located centrally in business headquarters and/or locally in your region. Local SMEs' input for the customization process should be obtained, if possible. Local SMEs would know your target audience better than central SMEs (Note: Local SMEs must have similar level of expertise on the subject). SMEs might serve a role as technical developers by writing necessary content, or assist technical developers by providing necessary skills and information. Also, if SME has proficiency of the language of the original course, he/she may be a translator.

Cultural Subject Matter Experts (CSMEs) provide culturally specific knowledge of the history, culture, society, environment, politics, economics and business of your region. Their input would be very useful in customizing courses that utilize the local environment and culture. You can consult various culturally knowledgeable people for your project, depending on the complexity or difficulty of cultural matters appearing in the course. Sometimes local SMEs or your peers in the office might play the role of CSMEs for a customization project.

Technical Developers develop and/or write content, case studies, games, and role plays, based on the customization design document with the guidance of a customization specialist. Technical developers could be played by SMEs, professional writers, or instructional designers, depending on the requirements and characteristics of the necessary content identified through the customization process.

Translators translate instructional materials as required, if your local language is not the same as the language used in the original courses. The translators should be evaluated and qualified, before you have them translate materials. Ideally, an SME would be the translator.

Training Administrator is responsible for arranging training sites, facilities, instructional hardware/software in the facilities, scheduling, and monitoring of conditions of facilities and hardware/software.

Production Specialists are responsible for production and reproduction of materials, in an event that your region has an in-house production department. A production department might include: (1) desktop publishing team for printed materials such as participant's guide, instructor's guide, handouts and transparencies; (2) video production team for audiovisual materials; and (3) computer software development team for computer-based instruction programs. If any of the production teams are not available in your region, you should locate and select an appropriate outside vendor for the production of materials. Depending on your organizational situation and availability of human resources, you should modify the configuration of a customization project team. In some situations, it is possible that some members of the team may serve several roles of functions. For instance, a translator might also be a cultural SME, and SME can be a technical developer as well.

Systematic Process of Customization: Overview

The following figure shows the main phases in the process of customization. Although the process is shown in a linear fashion, sub-steps in each phase could be conducted simultaneously by accomplishing the same activities. For instance, you should know the goals and objectives of the original course when you begin the customization process. The identification of goals and objectives occurs for customization needs assessment at first, it will later be used as part of the instructional design analysis. On the other hand, within a phase, sub-steps could be conducted in a different order, except some significant and pre-required steps, such as 'customization needs assessment' in the Analysis Phase and 'duplication of materials' in the Implementation Phase.

In the figure 2, this icon 🏃 indicates:

1. the first step of the whole process, which is Customization Needs Assessment in the analysis phase; and

2. Continuous Improvement as a part of the process, which should be in place for every phase.

It is important that the customization process should begin with an accurate needs assessment for the organization. Also, continuous improvement should be an ongoing effort throughout the whole customization process. Even the cases in which you have completed any phase of the process could contain the possibility of changes or new developments for your target audience, management decisions, learning environments, or other items related to your project. In those cases, you could always go back to any phase to which the new data are

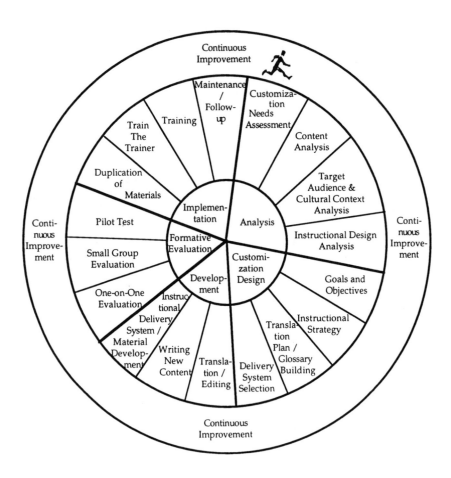

Figure 2: Model for transcultural customization of training programs

directly related, and revise your work as required. Although the improvement might not draw a linear graph over time, with continuous improvement in every step of the process, you can expect high quality instruction, participants' high achievement and customer satisfaction.

CHAPTER 3

Analysis for Customization

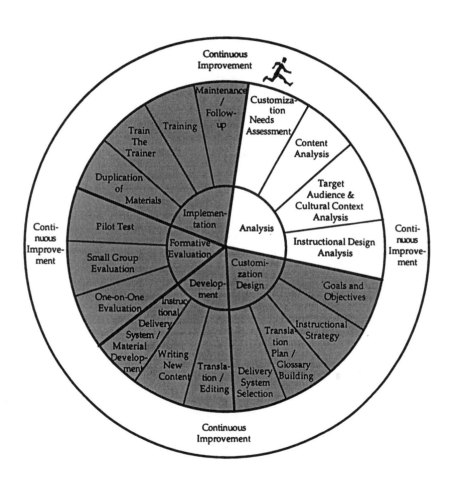

A successful customization for a local target audience starts with accurate analysis. The purpose of the analysis phase is to fully understand the original training program and every aspect of the local environment including participants, learning systems, etc., and to begin to think about how the program can be modified to be implemented in the local setting. The analysis should center around a local region. This phase includes: customization needs assessment, target audience analysis, content analysis, cultural context analysis and instructional design analysis.

CUSTOMIZATION NEEDS ASSESSMENT

Needs assessment is a proactive planning process for identifying needs, placing them in priority order and selecting the most important items for reduction or elimination (Kaufman, 1992). It is assumed that a local organization has identified needs. Customization needs assessment uses those needs as a starting point for determining whether the identified problems in the region can be resolved by a training course developed in other regions. The customization needs assessment helps the local organization to decide whether they can bring in a course developed in another region and customize it to address their needs or they should develop or outsource a new course to meet their needs.

The figure 3 presents a flow chart for a decision making process for the customization needs assessment.

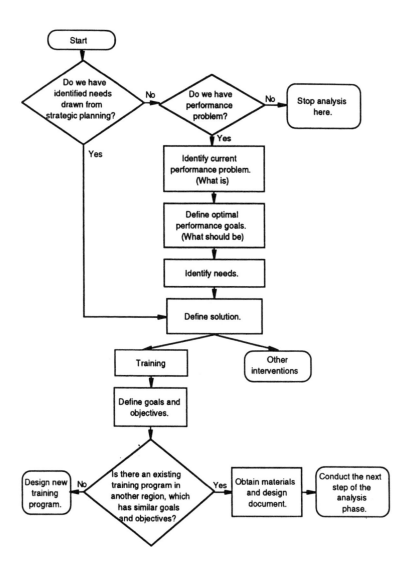

Figure 3: A decision making process of customization needs assessment.

Objectives

This step should be performed to achieve the following objectives:

- *Define the needs as they were addressed in the original course design document.*

It is important to look at the deep meanings of the course, such as why the course was developed and implemented. Sometimes you might find the course was developed because of very specific needs in that region which are quite different from your organizational needs. However, the course can be customized and then serve your own specific needs. For instance, if a course is intended to present a new strategy development technique, the original course would be focused on the details of strategy development process and 'how-to' types of explanations and exercises. But this course could be modified to meet your needs of strategic thinking development by presenting the overall process and the thinking behind the process which is not presented explicitly in the original course.

- *Determine whether the existing training course would be the solution for the regional needs.*

After you understand the needs for the original course, you are able to decide whether the course can be utilized in some way to resolve your local needs. Although the course was excellent for addressing the local participants, it might not be the right time to deliver it in your region or your participants may already have a deep understanding of the content the course is presenting. Therefore, The course may not need to be opened in the region.

- *Determine whether the course is mandatory for a specific target audience in the entire organization.*

When the course is mandatory for the all employees of an organization, no matter where they are located, the course should be delivered in your region as well. Even if it contains content or a delivery system which is not appropriate in your particular culture or organizational circumstances, you should value and understand the needs and objectives of the course and customize it to be suitable for the particular employees in your region.

- *Compare the approximate cost and cycle time of customizing an existing course to the cost and cycle time of designing a new course.*

A financial aspect of customization should be considered carefully. If your budget is limited for bringing in an existing course or the development of a new course costs less, you can decide to develop a course locally.

 Activities

To achieve any of the objectives in this step, you should collect enough detailed information and data, and analyze them thoroughly and systematically. Some of the activities involved in this step are:

- *Search internally and externally for appropriate course(s) to resolve the needs of your region.*

It is beneficial to have an organization wide system to share information on available courses in various regions. The organization can hold regular meetings to present each region's courses which are either completely developed or in the middle of development. These meetings would help each region to avoid duplication of similar course development. Active use of Internet is another way of keeping, sharing and sharing information among regions. In this case, user-friendly interface and language issues should be considered carefully. Depending on the organizational situation, the circulating of course profiles serves the purpose of sharing information on course development in regions.

- *Obtain course materials and design documents from the Original Instructional Designer (OID).*

If OID is not available, obtain materials from the training administrator in the region where the original course was developed and is currently being delivered. The design documents contain the organizational needs, objectives, target audiences, instructional strategy, delivery system specifications, course time table, course development plan and budget. All of this information is essential to understanding the course itself. It will give customization specialists insights into how useful the course could be in the local region, what degree the course should be customized, and how the course can be used after customization.

- *Review the original design document, focusing on needs assessment results and the description of course goals and objectives.*

The results of this activity will be used in all steps of the analysis phase. Goals and objectives of the original course are important data for content analysis.

- *Consult the Original Instructional Designer (OID), who conducted needs assessment and designed the original course, to identify the needs which lead to the development of the original course.*

It is most useful to have discussion with the original instructional designer, if he/she is available. The original designer can give you various information such as the reasons for course development, implicit course objectives which might not be shown in the design document, original target audiences' characteristics, and how the course took into consideration those characteristics, and so forth. He/she may give you some ideas as to where the course should be customized and where the course should not be customized from his/her own perspectives.

- *Attend a class or train-the-trainer session of the original course.*

By attending the class or train-the-trainer session of the original course, you could gather various data to answer many of the questions for each step of the analysis phase. So you should be cautious to collect all necessary data during the class. The activity expenses may be high if the course is taking place outside of your region; thus you should consider it in your budget planning.

- *Review the evaluation results of the original course.*

Evaluation results are another valuable resource for understanding the course. You can identify how much participants liked the course in which aspect, what level of learning participants achieved, what part of instruction was effective or ineffective in terms of learning, how much impact there was after the course was implemented, how easy it was for the participants to transfer their learning to their real life environment either at work or at their personal life, etc. This information can give you guidance on whether you can improve the course when you customize it for your region.

- *Review organization strategy and needs assessment results in your region.*

While you have to understand the original course extensively, your own organization strategy and needs assessment are extremely important, since your main purpose of delivering a training program is to resolve your local needs and organizational success reflecting your target audiences' performance.

- *Conduct cost-consequence analysis by comparing the cost of customizing the course to the cost of designing a new course.*

The whole process of launching a course should proceed within your budget. You should make a strategic decision whether a customization project or a new course development project is efficient. At the same time, you should also take into account resource availability in your region and the quality of instruction in both cases. The budget items and amount in each case will be different. For instance, if the original course uses a different language from yours, you should budget for language translation for the written materials and/or interpretation for course delivery. If you have to invite certified instructors for the course to be delivered in your region from outside of the region, you should consider their expenses as well.

 Questions Related to the Original Course

The following questions can be asked to guide your activities to identify and understand the needs of the original course:

- *What were the problems that led to design of the course?*

- *What were the stated goals and objectives for the course?*

- *Why was a training course selected as a solution?*

- *What were the organizational, operational, and individual needs underlying the course?*

- *Was the course effective for solving any problems in the organization?*

- *Is the course mandatory for every employee of the organization?*

- *Is the course mandatory for a certain population within the organization?*

 Questions Related to Your Region

The following questions can be asked to guide your activities for identifying and understanding the needs of your regional organization and to decide if an existing course would resolve your regional needs:

- *What are the identified needs in your region?*

- *What are the identified problems in your region?*

- *Is a training course the best solution for resolving the needs and problems in your region?*

- *Would the existing course be useful to address the needs of your region?*

- *In the event that your needs assessment results suggest developing a new course rather than to customize an existing course, is an instructional designer available for designing a new course?*

- *What is the budget estimated for the customization project and the budget for developing a new course for the same purposes, goals and objectives?*

- *What would be the cycle time of the course in your region?*

- *What are the indicators by which the course must be customized?*

- *What are customization problems? What will it cost to fix?*

- *Is it just a language problem? What are other problems?*

Team

To identify needs for customization of a course, the following roles of people should be involved in various ways:

- *Customization specialist*

A customization specialist has a major role for the entire process of the customization. He/she is responsible for the course to be customized. In this step, the person should gather a variety of information and data, and interview and discuss with stakeholders and the target audience of the course. Basically, the person initiates all activities described above with assistance from the following roles of people.

- *Original course-design Instructional Designer (OID)*

It is best if an original course-design instructional designer is available to discuss the history, organizational needs, and specific issues of the course. The information which the OID provides in this step will save the customization specialist's time and give insights and direction for conducting the project. However, the customization specialist should have his or her own reasoning process for understanding the course deeply and for making decisions on customization elements of the course.

- *Region management*

A region's own management will give the strategic direction for the course. The management team should provide implicit organizational needs and challenges so that educational or instructional interventions for resolving those issues can be identified. If the need for a training program is driven from the workplace, it is a customization specialist's role to challenge and persuade the management team to commit to sponsor the course. It is often the case that the course is successfully implemented and followed-up with meaningful transition from learning experience to work performance when the management team sees the value and supports the course since a learning intervention is not an ultimate solution to a performance problem. Rather, it is a beginning towards a resolution and an improvement of performance when we think about the whole work system. A system with an appropriate physical environment and feedback makes it possible for the participants to transfer their knowledge and skills obtained from the class and will make positive changes in participants' performance.

• *Corporate management, if required*

If the perceived needs for a course is not just a matter of regional organization, the corporate management should be involved in addressing the issue at the corporate level. Issues can be varied from criticality of utilization of corporate resources, such as budget and human resources for the customization project, to specific job tasks appeared in the customization target course.

Depending on the organizational culture, a communication style and a decision making process can be varied. In some cultures where seniority is valued within a hierarchical organizational structure, it might be the case that the region's management team takes charge of communicating with the corporate management. In another culture, the customization specialist might have full responsibility to communicate and resolve the issue with the corporate management team directly and more efficiently. Thus, it is another competency of a customization specialist to be more sensitive to the corporate and region's management culture and to communicate effectively.

• *Employees in work places where regional problems/needs are identified*

An existing course was developed for different target audiences in terms of culture even though their job is identical to region's target audience and features of identified performance problems are the same. To customize the course more effectively and make it culturally appropriate for the target audience in the region, employees' direct input is essential to find out whether the course has critical points which are not congruent with their own culture at work.

• *Possible consumers/customers*

One of the ultimate goals of a training program is to serve customers better through the performance of employees in an organization. If the objectives of the course is directly related to the customers, a way to improve the quality and cultural appropriateness of the course is to obtain opinions of potential customers in the region. Using various needs assessment techniques such as personal interviews, focus group interviews and surveys, you can find out whether the objectives of the course are comparable with what the local customers want and are relevant to their preference for the service and products your organization is providing.

 Resources

Resources which can provide basic information for the course and confirm the necessity and usefulness of an existing course include:

* *Original course materials and instructional design document*

* *Original needs assessment document*

* *Evaluation results of the original course*

* *Strategic planning document in your region*

* *Needs assessment document in your region*

The list above shows material resources. There are, of course, non-material resources needed, such as financial and human resources.

 Products

At the end of this step, you come to making a conclusion whether the customization project should proceed or not. It is important to document the customization needs assessment process. The products or outcome of this step include:

* *Decision on usefulness of the original course as a solution to the identified needs*

* *Customization needs assessment document*

CONTENT ANALYSIS

Content analysis is conducted to determine whether the existing content is consistent with a local version of the goals and objectives for the course, to identify the level of knowledge difficulty appropriate to the local target audience, and to determine if additional content and/or prerequisites are required for the local target audience to achieve the goals and objectives of the course.

 Objectives

- *Determine the level of specialty and difficulty of knowledge the course presents to your target audience.*

- *Identify prerequisites for your target audience to take the course.*

- *Determine whether additional prerequisite course(s) is required for your target audience.*

Sometimes the target audience doesn't have the basic knowledge and skills to take the customization target course, especially for the technology-related courses. If technology transfer from another region is critical for the performance of your region, you should carefully assess whether your target audience is ready to move on to the new technology. If not, the basic knowledge and skills should be understood by the participants before the original objectives are addressed. The prerequisite content can be provided as a separate course or imbedded in the course as a module, depending on the time allowance to take the course, urgency of delivery and the amount of prerequisite knowledge and skills to cover.

- *Determine the content area which should be customized and alternative supportive content which should be developed.*

After studying the original course materials, you should identify what should be customized. In many soft-skill-related courses, many parts of the contents contain culture-specific descriptions, examples, and activities. Look for where those parts are, and start to brainstorm whether it is customizable and how you can correct them to culturally fit with your target audience.

 Activities

- *Analyze content of materials and identify the content area which should be customized.*

Review the materials thoroughly. You might have to understand the overall content first, then look for cultural fitness. Have other team members review the materials as well to confirm your judgment.

- *Conduct a demo class with target audience using translated materials in the local language, if possible.*

A demo class could be conducted just the same as the original course, except using translated materials with your target audience in your region. A certified instructor should teach the course. In a demo class, you can get data (1) whether the target audience achieves the instructional goals and objectives as the course designed, (2) whether there is a gap between the knowledge of your target audience and the prerequisite of the course, and (3) whether the context of the content, such as examples and learning activities, are appropriate for your target audience and learning environment. During the demo class, you could also identify your target audience's characteristics and attitude, and locate areas to customize, which will be used in the analysis of target audience and cultural context. Also, you can find out how your target audience reacts to the details of the course, such as use of humor, graphics, games, and cast and background situation in video materials in terms of cultural acceptance or denial. It might be better for you to observe the class and to have an instructor to teach the class so that you can have a better idea about the course, i.e., content, target audience, and learning environment. Note that conducting a demo class is different from conducting formative evaluation. A demo class is for testing the original course with your target audience rather than testing customized course for revisions which should be conducted later on in the process of customization.

Translated materials used at this step are different from the ones which would be produced at the end of the transcultural customization project. Here, you can use literally translated materials, i.e., materials not yet customized, to find elements of customization of the course. If translated materials are not available at this time, you could run a demo class in your language using the materials used in the original course which might be written or recorded in a foreign language only if your target audience can read and comprehend the original materials in an acceptable level.

- *Identify the level of knowledge specialty and difficulty of the content for your target audience.*

Based on the review of the instructional design document of the original course, determine the prerequisite or required entry behavior of the participants. If your target audience does not have the required entry behavior for the course, you should consider customizing the course by covering the prerequisite in the beginning of the course. If the original course design document is not available, you could consult the instructional designer of the original course and/or base on your notes and judgment from the original course or train-the-trainer (TTT) class you have attended to understand the original target audience and to obtain other necessary information.

 Questions

Some of the questions you can ask to analyze the content of the course include:

- *What prerequisites are identified in the original instructional design document?*

- *What are the necessary prerequisites for your target audience based on their knowledge and the skills level of the course?*

- *Is the content highly technical to which your target audience has never been exposed before? If so, is there any prerequisite course available?*

- *Which additional content that should be added?*

- *Who were the subject matter experts for designing the original course? Is a local SME available?*

 Team

The following are the roles for conducting content analysis:

- *Customization specialist*

- *Local SME(s)*

He or she can provide expertise on the subject to determine whether the customization target course is understandable for the target audience in the region. If a local SME is not available, consult the most knowledgeable person(s) in the content area or relevant job area, and the original SME(s). Having a supportive relationship with the local SME is important for the whole customization project, since he or she can provide specific comments about the subject matter and write new content as a part of the customized course.

* *A sample of target audience, if you run a demo class*

Resources

Required resources for content analysis are:

* *Original design document*

* *Original training materials*

* *Translated materials, if available and if you run a demo class*

* *A certified instructor, if you run and observe a demo class*

Products

The final product of content analysis is a description of the requirements for the content customization.

TARGET AUDIENCE & CULTURAL CONTEXT ANALYSIS

Target audience analysis is conducted to identify a local target audience's characteristics and to determine if they have the prerequisites required to take the course. A customization specialist should compare the analysis results with the original course's target audience analysis results. The results of this step help to identify elements of the existing course, to customize prerequisites for participants to take the course, and to customize the course accordingly.

In addition to the target audience analysis, cultural context analysis should be conducted to examine the context of the course, such as the cultural aspects of the content area, themes, learning activities, and examples. A customization specialist should examine these in terms of value orientation, customs and beliefs.

Areas of Target Audience Analysis

Target audience analysis can be done in the following four areas: learning styles, learner characteristics, job classification, and basic demographics.

Learning style is a consistent pattern of behavior and performance by which an individual approaches educational experiences. It is a composite of cognitive, affective, and physiological behaviors that serves as relatively stable indicators of how a learner perceives, interacts with, and responds to the learning environment. It is formed in the deep structure of neural organization and personality that is molded by individual human development and the cultural experiences of home, school, and society (Zintel, 1995).

For instance, Dunn, Dunn, and Price (In Zintel, 1995) identify 22 variables in the way people learn within five categories of stimuli; (1) environmental (i.e., sound, light, temperature, and design), (2) emotional (i.e., motivation, persistence, responsibility, and structure), (3) sociological (i.e., self, pair, peers, team, adult, and varied), (4) physiological (i.e., perceptual, intake, time, and mobility), and (5) psychological (i.e., global vs. analytic, hemisphericity, impulsive vs. reflective, and simultaneous vs. successive psychological process).

David Kolb's learning styles model (In Zintel, 1995) is another example, which is based on experiential learning theory. He categorizes four learning styles: accomodator, diverger, converger and assimilator. Depending on the learning style, learning methodology could be differentiated. For instance, accomodators learn best from new experiences, games, discussion and interaction; on the other hand, divergers learn best from lectures, readings, research and observation.

Although everyone in a culture does not have the same learning style, there are cultural group differences, which can be generalized in a group based on the individual's cultural and educational background. For instance, many Koreans are used to structured, lecture style instruction with less class participation while many Americans are used to less structured instruction with active class participation.

Learner characteristics are general characteristics that participants bring to the course of instruction, such as reading levels, attention span, previous experience, motivational levels, attitudes toward work, performance levels in previous instructional or working situations, and extent and context of related knowledge and skills that participants already possess (Dick & Carey, 1990).

Job classification includes business units they belong to, specific jobs and/or titles such as engineers, technicians, sales and marketing professionals, finance specialists, accountants, planning specialists and HRD professionals, and positions such as line operators, supervisors, managers, senior managers, and executives. Depending on their jobs and positions, people tend to have different characteristics and learning styles. For instance, finance and account people might enjoy specific analysis of problems while sales and marketing people like more tactical information. Executives might require more holistic understanding of content where supervisors need more specific cases and instruction. It seems there are not many cultural differences within specific job functions in different cultures. The different learning characteristics may be coming from their jobs rather than their culture. However, in some national culture or organizational culture, this is not the case. Although people in the same jobs, based on their culture, their learning preferences and styles could be varied. You should identify and take into account your local target audience's leaning characteristic depending on their jobs and positions.

Basic demographics include the target audience's educational background, age, gender, race, ethnicity, nationality, language, religion, and physical location. It is important to adjust the difficulty of the content and the use of language to the local target audience's level of educational background.

In some cultures, it is a taboo to have males and females in the same room. In other cultures, it is not wise to have different age groups in one classroom. If the culture highly values seniority, young participants may not participate actively in the class activities in the presence of their boss or elderly people. Or, in just opposite to that, the senior people might keep quiet to see how young people generate their opinions. Sometimes it might be better to have participants come together at one site rather than send an instructor to each location. Sometimes it works best the other way around. Depending on the objectives of the course, culturally appropriate participant configuration is necessary.

Objectives

The major objectives of this step can be summarized as follows:

- *Identify predominate learning style of the target audience in your region.*

- *Identify predominate learner characteristics of the target audience in your region.*

- *Identify the job classification of the target audience in your region as well as in the original course.*

- *Determine if those job/task analysis results are exactly the same with the job/task in your region.*

- *Identify the basic demographics of the target audience in your region.*

- *Identify environmental, cultural, social, political, and other relevant data of the original course.*

This objective includes miscellaneous backgrounds such as measurement system, currency, working hours, common living expenses, weather, names and job titles. For instance, if a management course includes a case of a country's traditional management style as a bad example and suggests a new management style for today's business world, it is wise to address the objective for the future management style they should pursue with specific data logically presented so that it can be accepted by the participants.

- *Determine the relevance of the content to your target audience, regional working environment, business environment and organizational structure, and the historical/economical/social background of your culture.*

- *Determine the areas, if any, which should be customized based on the target audience's learning style, learner characteristics, job, other demographic characteristics, and cultural context.*

For instance, if your target audience is familiar with descriptive textbook style of explanations in instructional materials rather than intensive bullet-points-style of explanations, you might want to develop a descriptive Participants' Guide.

- *Identify what absolutely cannot be used from the original course with your target audience.*

- *Identify what might be tried, although your target audience may not be familiar with it, and what fits without any cultural acceptance problem.*

 Activities

There are many activities for analyzing your target audience and cultural context for the course in your region. Some of examples are:

- *Interview and survey the target audience to identify learner characteristics.*

A continuous effort for this activity is required until you have a good sense to understand the characteristics of employees in your region. Also, this activity does not have to be formal. Informal conversation over coffee or tea with various people in the organization would help you understand and identify their characteristics as learners.

- *Observe people working and in training.*

- *Use data gathering instruments to identify your target audience.*

For instance, you could use Kolb's learning-style inventory (Kolb, 1976) to assess your target audience's learning style.

- *Consult other designers in your region to share lessons learned regarding learning styles and characteristics.*

- *Train your target audience to be more effective learners with various learning strategies.*

This objective might not be directly related to the customization project. However, it is helpful to understand the trends of instructional technology and learning activities which appear effective in practice and what are the new required behaviors for the future of the organization. Then you can help the employees to be prepared for the

new behaviors through learning activities they are involved in.
Customized courses can offer opportunities to change your target
audiences' behaviors and attitudes.

- *Review job/task analysis results from the design document of the
  original program.*

- *Identify target audience's basic demographics by reviewing
  employees' profile, their current location, etc.*

- *Review results from a demo class conducted at the content analysis
  step.*

- *Identify contextual differences and similarities between the culture
  where the original course was designed and your culture by
  reviewing course materials and notes from the original class and/or
  train-the-trainer session.*

- *Consult your cultural subject matter expert (CSME).*

As a customization specialist, if you are from the same cultural
background as your target audience, you might have general insights
about your own culture. If the course requires specific historical or
cultural knowledge that you are unsure of, consult more knowledgeable
person(s) in cultural context matters. You might be able to find CSMEs
at local academic or social institutions. Depending on the cultural issue
you are dealing with, CSME(s) might be colleagues, neighbors,
children, school teachers, journalists, sociology/anthropology/history
professors in local colleges and universities, or professional culturalists.

- *Study your own culture, including its society, politics, history, and
  environment.*

This activity should be an ongoing effort and process for you as a
customization specialist. Specific activities may include networking
with CSMEs, reading local newspapers and journals regularly, reading
professional journals and books related to the local and other cultures,
observing other training classes and work places, observing various
things around you and socializing with your target audiences.

Questions

The guiding questions for analysis in this step are:

- *Who is the major target audience in your region?*
- *What learning styles do they have?*
- *What learner characteristics do they have?*
- *What learning activities do they like and feel comfortable to participate in?*
- *What comments did they make on evaluation forms in other training courses?*
- *What is their attention span for a class?*

Use your experience with your target audience or consider the usual meeting hours and high school class hours in your culture.

- *Which business units do they belong to?*
- *What are their jobs?*
- *Where are they located?*
- *Which cultures were considered in designing the original course?*
- *Which languages were identified for translation of the course?*
- *Are customization guidelines for the course available?*

If the original course is designed with plans for the future customization, there should be some guidelines for customization. If the guidelines are available, you should obtain them and study whether the suggestions are applicable in your region.

- *What should be customized for your target audience in terms of learning activities, class size, group activity, instructional media, instructional delivery method, gender, job title, job classification, and age composition of class?*
- *Is your target audience familiar with the general description/explanation, examples, case studies, contents of games and role plays? Are there any graphics included in the material(s)?*

Are these relevant to your working environment, business environment, organizational structure and historical/economical/societal backgrounds of your culture?

For instance, in Western cultures, employees are paid and promoted according to their performance. Some Asian cultures, however, still maintain a 'pay by seniority' system. If the original course has an example of payment for performance which is not your region's payment system, you should identify basic cultural differences on the issue and find out the best way to resolve this difference.

- *Is the humor and folk tales understandable by your target audience? If not, do not translate it word by word, rather, delete it or recreate humor which can be understood by your target audience.*

- *What are reactions of your target audience in a demo class in terms of cultural acceptance and denial?*

 Team

The following roles are key to analyze target audience and cultural context. Actual people who are involved in this step could be different depending on their availability and the organizational situation for the project.

- *Customization specialist*

- *A sample group from the target audience*

- *CSME(s)*

- *A certified instructor, if you run a demo class*

 Resources

To be able to perform the activities to achieve in this step, you can utilize the following resources, if they are available:

- *Original training materials*

- *Original target audience analysis results*

- *Target audience's job description*

- *Translated materials, if available and if you run a demo class*

 Products

If you successfully finished this step, you would have target audience analysis description and cultural customization requirements.

INSTRUCTIONAL DESIGN ANALYSIS

Instructional design analysis is conducted to identify whether the instructional design elements of the original course are suitable for the local target audience and learning environment. The instructional design elements which should be identified in this step include analyses of goals and objectives of the course, instructional strategy, learning environment and instructional delivery system, instructional materials design and development, transferability of learning outcome into workplace, and evaluation strategy and time availability.

Some of the elements here could have been identified in previous steps of the analysis phase. If you have reached this step, having completed previous steps in the analysis phase in this document, you should already have identified goals and objectives of the original course in the customization needs assessment step. In this case, you could just review the goals and objectives of the original course for the purpose of instructional design analysis.

This step is focused on the analysis of instructional design of the original course. More specific description of general instructional design elements will be presented in the next chapter.

 Objectives

Analyzing the original course's instructional design should achieve the following objectives:

- *Identify goals and objectives of the original course.*

- *Identify instructional strategy of the original course.*

- *Identify instructional materials used for the original course, including participant's guide, instructor's guide and other print-based or non-print-based materials.*

- *Identify instructional delivery system used for the original course, such as instructor-led course using video equipment, computer-based instruction, multimedia-based instruction using CD-ROM and computers, and individualized instruction using print-based materials.*

- *Identify evaluation method(s) and level(s) incorporated in the original course.*

- *Identify whether the outcome of the instruction could be transferred to the working environment in your region.*

- *Identify the areas which should be customized for your target audience, including instructional strategy, delivery system, material design/ development specifications, and evaluation method(s) and level(s), based on your target audience's characteristics, demographics, and resource availability in your region.*

- *Identify the level of support your target audience gets from their managers or supervisors.*

- *Identify the physical and social context of workplace in which the knowledge and skill will be used by target audience.*

- *Identify how relevant the skills covered in the course are to the workplace in your region.*

- *Identify whether the course is designed for the target audience to transfer their knowledge and skills to the workplace.*

- *Identify the areas of customization to increase transferability of training into the workplace by your target audience, considering managerial or supervisor support, physical and social aspects of the working environment, and relevance of skills to workplace.*

 Activities

- *Review design document.*

- *Consult the original instructional designer.*

- *Review and compare instructor's guide, participant's guide, and other materials at the same time.*

- *Review evaluation results and any available evaluation reports of the original course classes.*

- *Interview target audience and their managers / supervisors to find out what and how much support the target audience gets from managers and supervisors.*

- *Observe the workplace and interview the target audience to find out the physical and social aspects of the working environment.*

 Questions

Identify the instructional design elements by asking following questions:

Goals and objectives

- *What were the goals and objectives?*

Instructional strategy

- *What was the instructional strategy in the original course?*

- *What are the implications from the Target Audience and Cultural Context Analysis results in your region?*

- *Which instructional strategy from the original course would work for your target audience?*

- *What additional instructional strategies would work for your target audience?*

- *What were instructional activities in the original course, such as small group discussion, class presentation, games, role plays, lecture, watching video, individual study, and structured on-the-job training?*

- *What are the instructional activities in which your target audience feels comfortable to participate?*

- *Which instructional activities should be changed for your target audience?*

Instructional delivery system

- *What was the original course's instructional delivery system?*

- *What resources are required from the original course for customization?*

- *If the original instructional delivery system is not available in your region, what are the alternatives?*

- *What are the specifications, advantages, and disadvantages for each delivery system?*

Examples of delivery system include computer-based training (CBT), video, audio, overheads, handouts, and various distance learning system. You should identify the specification for each delivery system. For instance, in case of CBT, you should identify the types (Macintosh or IBM compatibles) of computer used, speed, memory size and operating system of the computer, application software used, and number of computers required.

- *Which are the delivery systems you are able and can afford to develop?*

- *Are good quality outside vendors or internal production teams available to produce the instructional material for a specific delivery system?*

- *In the case of classroom delivery, what are instructor specifications?*

- *Who are the possible instructors and a possible master instructor in your region?*

Instructional material design/development

- *What are the identified requirements to develop and produce instructional materials?*

- *How easily are the original course materials customized?*

Transfer of learning

- *Will new skills in the workplace be encouraged, recognized, and praised or discouraged, ignored, and punished?*

- *How culturally appropriate are the new skills in your regional workplace?*

- *Will the use of the new skills depend upon equipment, facilities, tools, timing, or other resources? And, does your region provide those necessary resources?*

- *How is the target audience supposed to share the knowledge and skills with their peers, supervisors and/or subordinates in the original course design? Is it also appropriate in your region?*

For example, suppose that a course is designed for participants to present or demonstrate the content of the training to the other people in the workplace. In a diffuse culture, in which people tend to consider work and private life as closely linked, people might consider training as a personal benefit or incentive so that they have no intention of sharing the new knowledge and skills in their workplace. In this case, you might want to design a formal assignment for participants to distribute the new knowledge and skills to their peers, superiors, and subordinates. On the other hand, in a specific culture where people tend to split work and private life, they consider training as a part of their job. So, they have more intention to share the new knowledge and skills in the workplace. In this case, an informal direction of sharing information with peers during the training sessions might be appropriate.

Evaluation

- *What levels of evaluation does the original course have?*

- *To what extent do the levels of evaluation fit in your regional situation?*

 Resources

You will heavily rely on and analyze the design document, original instructional materials, and results from a demo class.

Products

You will have instructional design customization requirements after you have analyzed the instructional design of the original course.

 Continuous Improvement

Don't forget about Continuous Improvement. Ask yourself if there is other information or data available which could affect the analysis phase. Accurate analysis is the key to the whole process of customization. You should have the analysis results document by now, which describes areas of customizations based on the customization needs assessment, content analysis, target audience and cultural context analysis, and instructional design analysis.

CHAPTER 4

Customization of Instructional Design

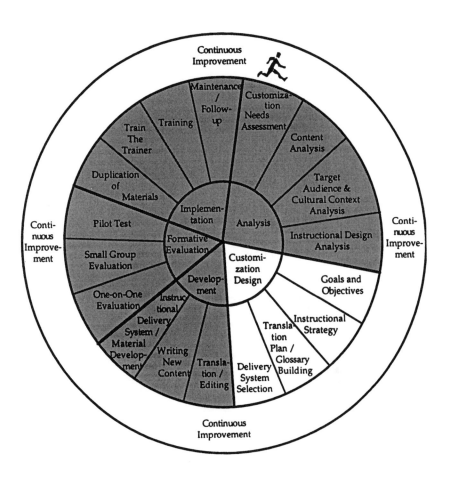

In the customization design phase, a customization specialist designs a customized course mainly by developing a customization design document, based on the products of the analysis phase. He or she also starts to plan for translation if translation is required in the local region.

Before we begin to explore the customization design, let's look at the general instructional elements which are an important base for customization design.

Elements of Instructional Design

Goals and objectives indicate who the target audience is, what they are expected to perform at the end of the course, how you would know whether they achieve the goals and objectives, and under what condition the performance will be observed. For measurable objectives, you could find the following elements of ABCD in the objective statements: (A) audience, (B) behavior, (C) condition, and (D) data or criteria to be used to calibrate success.

Instructional strategy describes the general components of a set of instructional materials and the procedures that will be used with those materials to elicit particular learning outcomes from participants (Dick & Carey, 1990). Major components of an instructional strategy include:

1. pre-instructional activities, such as introduction of the course, trainer and participants;

2. information presentation for actual content area;

3. participants' participation for drill and/or practice;

   Participants' participation can be designed around instructional activities, such as small and large group discussion, presentation, role plays, simulations, games and dialogues.

4. evaluation, such as paper and pencil test and presentation; and

5. closing.

Learning environment is where instruction takes place. The learning environment should be designed carefully to enhance participants' learning process and achievement levels. Physical conditions of facilities, such as room temperature, seating arrangement for classroom activities, light, and sound, should be considered. In addition, an appropriate supply and use of instructional hardware and software should be analyzed. If the course is not conducted in a classroom setting, for instance using Internet as a distance learning course, the design of the Internet course itself should be analyzed whether it is well structured with easy to follow instructions. The distance learning course is also closely related to the issue of instructional delivery system.

Instructional delivery system is more directly related to instructional hardware and software, such as print-based materials, overhead projectors with transparency materials, computer systems for Computer-Based Training (CBT) and Internet-based instruction, and VCR players and tapes for an individualized learning environment. The selection of instructional delivery system should be done through the analysis of cost effectiveness, cost efficiency, and availability of a system in your region. Depending on the instructional delivery system, which is a vehicle to deliver instruction to participants, learning environment design could be different. For instance, a classroom environment can be used for conventional style of classroom activities and lecture. The participants' workplace can be used for on-the-job training (OJT), while each participant's office or home can be used for individualized lessons. Furthermore, the computer lab or each participant's desk top computer can be used for CBT and Internet-based instruction.

Instructional material design and development are based on the instructional strategy. For conventional classroom courses, instructional materials include the participant's guide (PG), instructor's guide (IG), level 1 evaluation forms, level 2 evaluation material(s), and other materials for class activities and presentation.

At this step, you should identify material development requirements for each item and locate an original version of material(s) for possible duplication. For instance, consider the following:

1. Print-based materials: page layout and writing style (descriptive vs. bullet points)

2. Video material: cast, sound channel (separation of narration and background music), video and audio quality for duplication, and availability of the master tape and scripts

3. CBT: compatibility and availability of computer hardware and software, source files availability for customization, possibility of any modification or change of programming or authoring, and in-house or contracting programming capability for modification

Evaluation methods include paper-and-pencil test, presentations, speeches, case study assessment, final report, observation, and survey. An appropriate evaluation method(s) should be selected depending on the required behavior indicated in the goals and objectives statement.

Levels of evaluation are categorized with the following levels based on measuring: (1) participants' reaction to the course to identify whether or not they liked the course and how they would make changes in the next training, (2) participants' achievement to identify whether they achieved the goals and objectives of the course, (3) participants' transfer of learning to their work to identify whether they have applied what they have learned in the course to their routine work in the organization, (4) return on investment to identify whether the course was an effective and efficient financial investment for the organization. Most courses include levels one and two. Levels three and four should be determined based on the course characteristics and the management decision.

Transferability of learning outcome into the workplace is critical since the main purpose of training is to solve any problems or to resolve any needs of the workplace. You should consider whether the training course, which you have been considering and analyzing for possible delivery in your region, could be customized for your target audience for transferring the knowledge and skills they learn during the training courses into their workplaces.

You should consider transferability of training into the workplace in terms of the managerial support the target audience can have, conditions of physical and social aspects of learning and working environments, and relevance of skills to the workplace (Dick & Carey, 1996).

A customization design document is like a design document for developing a new course. A customization specialist should create the following for the customized course:

• Goals and objectives;

- Instructional strategy;
- Learning environment/instructional delivery system description;
- Evaluation plan (with test items, if required);
- Translation plan; and
- Implementation plan.

To move through this phase, you should carefully review your instructional design customization requirements. These requirements reflect your work on the analysis phase, and will guide generation of the customization design document.

 Objectives
- *Restate goals and objectives.*

Most likely the goals and objectives of the original course would remain the same in the customized course. You can just restate those goals and objectives in this phase for the customization design document. If you create totally new goals and objectives here, it is a new course design project rather than a customization project.

- *Design learning strategies to accommodate predominate learning styles of your target audience.*

In the analysis phase, you have analyzed the learning styles of your target audience. The results should be applied here for designing appropriate learning strategies. Sometimes it is useful to use new learning strategies which are not familiar to your target audience. Those new strategies would give participants motivation to get involved in the learning activities. Especially, those who have taken various courses offered in the organization might experience similar activities and get bored with them. They would enjoy new challenges in the learning activities. You should always keep in mind that the learning strategies should be designed for participants to actively participate in learning and to achieve the goals and objectives of the course.

- *Modify existing instructional strategy and/or develop new instructional strategy.*

Instructional strategy provides a structure of the entire course. It shows the flow of the presentation which should be logically planned to achieve the objectives. Various motivational activities should be embedded in the instructional strategy. Motivational instruction has four elements: attention, relevance, confidence, and satisfaction (Keller, 1987a; 1987b). The instruction should have some elements which can bring participants' attention, such as interesting new stories, funny jokes, games, pictures, physical exercise, etc. which participants have not exposed before or do not anticipate to happen. The content of the course and all examples should be relevant to participants, even for the jokes. When the context of learning is relevant to participants, they pay more attention to the presentation and actively participate in learning activities. And most of all they learn better and more quickly. Participants should feel confident that they can achieve the objectives of the course and pass any exams or challenges which the course provides and which their jobs and tasks require them to perform. At last, participants should be satisfied about the course in terms of their learning achievement level, job relevance, enjoyment of learning activities, and cooperation with other participants and instructor. These elements should be considered to motivate participants with the instructional strategy so that they can learn more effectively with full participation, involvement, and concentration.

- *Determine learning environment and instructional delivery system based on your target audience's characteristics, demographics, and resource availability of your region.*

The learning environment as a physical context should be determined by considering the target audience's learning style and the availability and capacity of instructional hardware and software in your region. If your regional learning environment and hardware/software are limited compared to those of the original course, you have to customize the course appropriately to your learning environment and hardware/software available at the point of time the course will be delivered to your target audience in your region.

- *Determine evaluation levels and methods.*

The same evaluation levels and methods as the original course are used most likely for the customized course. However, each evaluation test item should be reviewed to determine whether the test items are appropriate to your customized course. It is important to measure what participants have experienced and learned in the training programs.

- *Identify translation requirements and develop translation guide.*

The translation process should be planned in the design phase, because translation is one of the key elements for the customization project if the languages in your region and the region the course was originally developed are different. Also, the translation process itself takes time to conduct. Since a language is a basic vehicle for communication, the appropriate and comprehensive uses of language are so important to understand the concepts and knowledge presented in a course. Careful and perfect translation is critical.

Translation requirements include: (1) materials that should be translated, (2) portions of the content that will be translated, (3) the language into which the materials will be translated, (4) translation guidelines for culture-specific content including translation glossary which consists of identified vocabularies, their definitions, and translated words in your language, and (5) translation timelines. The translation guidelines also include an organization specific terms, such as organizational philosophy, vision statements, business units, titles, and major product names, etc.

It is a good translation plan to have professional editors for grammatical editing and to have SME and/or CSME for content verification of the translation.

- *Identify qualified translator(s).*

The quality of translation depends on the quality of translators. It might be beneficial in a long term to invest on training certified translators in your organization. As much as they are knowledgeable about the languages used in your organization, their translation will maintain high quality.

- *Determine implementation requirements for the course.*

If your region has a responsible person for training administrations such as registration, class time scheduling, room assignment, and equipment arrangement, you should communicate with a training administrator for the implementation plan. Although you would determine specific delivery dates and location later, you should consult the training administrator in advance to identify the implementation requirements.

In case of Internet-based instruction and computer-based instruction, the implementation requirements are quite different from classroom learning interventions. Internet-based instruction should have a web master who is responsible for the design, development, maintenance and update of the course homepage and a learning facilitator who is responsible for the content areas and facilitates on-line participants' various learning activities and inquiries. The specific responsibilities of these people should be identified and agreed upon among each other for developing the implementation plan.

The other aspect of the implementation plan is promotion of the course. The course opening information should be announced in the organization so that target audience can take the course. The promotion plan includes course title, business needs, goals and objectives, target audience, pre-requisites, outlines of the course content, class size, time schedule, course fees, and registration method and deadlines. The course promotion plan items are identical for any courses whether it is a customized or newly developed course. In many large organizations, they publish the course profiles annually with the information described as a promotion plan above. It is also easy to find many organizations who have an electronic system for course information and registration. Based on the system your organization has, the customization specialist should prepare and provide information on the implementation of the course in this step.

 Activities

Major activities to achieve the objectives of this phase include:

- *Identify or develop goals and objectives of the customized course.*

- *Modify or redesign instructional strategy.*

- *Modify or redesign instructional delivery system and learning environment.*

- *Modify or redesign evaluation levels and methods for the course.*

- *Consult a translation process expert, if available.*

- *Find and/or build a glossary for the terms used in the course.*

- *Contact possible translator(s) and translation verifier(s).*

- *Develop translation guide for translators, verifiers and editors.*

- *Plan course implementation, including identification of master instructor and instructor candidates, train-the-trainer (TTT) schedule, training schedule, and training facility.*

- *Develop customization design document.*

- *Revise customization design document, as required.*

 Questions

Questions for conducting design of customization course are listed in each design elements as follows:

Instructional strategy

- *What instructional strategies would work for your target audience to achieve the objectives?*

- *What are identified learning activities with which your target audience would feel comfortable participating?*

- *What are new learning activities with which your target audience would find challenging and motivating?*

- *Which instructional activities can you use as they are in the original course, including small group discussion, class presentation, games, role plays, lecture, video watch, individual study, and structured OJT?*

- *How would you optimize the instructional sequence of the course, including breaks, lunch, pre-work, and assignments?*

- *What kinds of motivational elements were used in the original course and how will they be used in the customized course?*

Learning environment/instructional delivery system description

- *What instructional delivery systems are available in your region?*

- *Which delivery system would be most effective and efficient to deliver the customized course?*

- *What are the specifications for each delivery system and material development system such as computer-based instruction, Internet-based instruction, computer presentation, video, audio, overhead projector materials, and handouts?*

- *Which delivery systems can you afford financially and be able to develop technically?*

- *Can you hire high quality outside vendors to produce the instructional material for a specific delivery system? If not, what are the alternatives?*

- *In case of classroom delivery, what are the qualifications for instructors and facilitators?*

Evaluation plan

- *What levels of evaluation would be appropriate and necessary for the course in your region?*

- *How would you measure participants' learning achievement in the course?*

- *How would you measure participants' learning transfer to their work?*

- *Are question items appropriate for measuring your participants achievement on the customized goals and objectives?*

- *What would be the evaluation questions for 4 levels of evaluation?*

Translation plan

- *Which materials should be translated?*

- *Which parts of the content should be translated, the entire content or part of the content?*

- *Which language should be used for translating the materials?*

- *Who are qualified translators and editors?*

- *Is translation glossary available?*

- *What are identified vocabularies, their definitions and translated words in your language which should be included in the translation glossary?*

- *What are required guidelines for translation of culture-specific and organization-specific content?*

- *When should the translation be completed?*

- *Who and how will the translation be verified?*

Implementation Plan

- *How many participants do you anticipate enrolling?*

- *How many times should the course be offered?*

- *Who is the master instructor or facilitator?*

- *How many instructors and facilitators are required?*

- *Who are best possible instructors and facilitators?*

- *How and when will the instructors and facilitators be trained for the course implementation?*

- *By when should all the target population complete the course?*

- *Where should the course be offered?*

- *What are other implementation specifications such as class sizes, class settings, transportation and accommodation for participants, and materials which should be provided to the participants other than in-class instructional materials?*

- *What is a promotion plan of the course to announce and recruit participants?*

Team

To design the customized course, a customization specialist who has expertise in instructional design should perform the major role with cooperation of a translation process expert and a training administrator if they are available in the organization. In many real project situations, it is common that the customization specialist performs all roles of instructional designer, translation process expert, and administrator.

 Resources

Resources required to design the customized course are:

- *Customization needs assessment result document*

- *Target audience analysis document*

- *Content customization requirements*

- *Cultural context customization requirements*

- *Instructional design customization requirements*

- *Original course materials*

 Products

The customization design phase ends with the customization design document and translation guidelines which will be basic resources for the next phase, customization program development.

 Continuous Improvement

Confirm that: (1) the goals and objectives are well maintained from the original course to resolve your regional and organizational needs; (2) the instructional strategy is well modified to fit closely with your target audience's learning style and culture; (3) the translation plan is feasible; and (4) the delivery system is appropriately selected reflecting your regional situation.

CHAPTER 5
Development of Customized Instruction

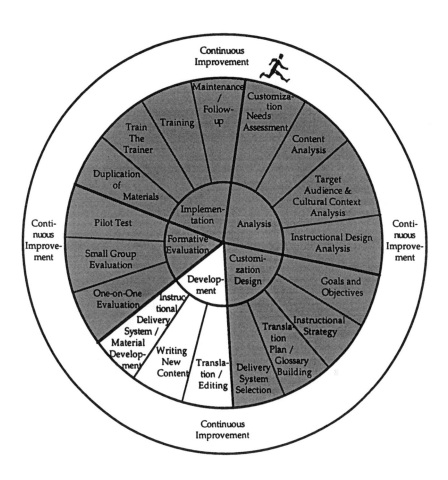

In this phase, a customization specialist actually develops instructional materials and systems that he or she has designed in the previous customization design phase. Major steps of this phase include: Translation and editing, writing of new content, and instructional delivery system and material development.

TRANSLATION & EDITING

Translation is one of the most critical steps to having quality materials. Depending on the local organizational situation, a customization specialist should train translator(s).

For an effective translation process, the customization specialist should have translators attend the basic courses which introduce a management philosophy and/or history of the organization. Those courses would help translators to understand the company and the course better.

 Objectives

There is only one simple objective for translating materials: Translate and edit the materials.

 Activities

Although the objective is simple, the process of translation requires hard work. The process includes the following activities:

- *Build translation glossary and guidelines.*

- *Have translator(s) and editor(s) translate and edit the materials according to the translation guidelines.*

- *Review the translated and edited materials.*

- *Have local SME(s), if available, review translated materials to ensure the accuracy of the translation and the proper use of terms in the content.*

- *Have CSME(s) review translated materials to ensure cultural appropriateness.*

- *Have another translator translate the translated material back into original target language to check for accuracy, if possible.*

For the translation of audio and video materials, it is best to obtain the scripts, and provide them to the translator(s) with the materials. If materials are videos, you should direct the translator(s) whether the audio will be dubbed or captioned so that translator(s) can consider the use of language appropriately either to fit in a chunk of frames with the captioned written sentences or to synchronize with the lips of actors and actresses with dubbed audio. You might have to have differently experienced translators for those different formats. If materials are computer-based lessons, you can provide either printed screens, a screen design portion of the storyboard, or the CBI lessons themselves to the translator(s).

 Questions

The following questions guide the customization specialist to confirm the quality of translation:

- *Are the materials translated correctly in terms of grammar, vocabulary, sentence structure, etc.?*

- *Are terms correctly and consistently translated?*

- *Is the translated language comprehensible and easy to understand?*

- *Are humor appropriately translated?*

- *How well does the translator follow the translation guidelines, especially for the organization and management specific terms?*

- *Do translated materials contain culturally appropriate meanings and contents?*

 Team

A customization specialist monitors the translation process. Translators and editors play essential roles in this step. Also, the contribution of subject matter experts in translated content verification insures the quality of translation and content presentation in the materials.

 Resources

- *Original course material(s) including scripts for audio/video materials*

- *Translation guidelines including translation glossary*

 Products

At the end of this step, you will have completely translated and edited materials. These materials will be further developed in selected media formats later in this phase.

WRITING NEW CONTENTS

Based on the customization design requirements, a customization specialist may have to have new contents written. The new contents would include prerequisite information for the course, customized games or role plays, examples, new evaluation test items, etc. Depending on the customization design requirements and availability of SMEs and technical developers in the region, the customization specialist can have them write the new contents. The new contents should be well integrated with other parts of the course which is designed in another culture.

This step can be proceeded simultaneously with the translation and editing step.

 Objectives

- *Write necessary contents of the material in local language, based on the customization design document.*

 Activities

- *Have local SMEs or technical developers write any necessary content.*

- *Have other SMEs review new content for its accuracy.*

You may want to develop guidelines for expert review, including descriptions of course goals and objectives, and explanation of how the new contents fit with the entire course, other courses, or curriculum.

 Team

It is common to have internal or external experts write any necessary new contents for subject based on specific knowledge and skills.

Depending on the types of content, a technical developer should write games, role plays or video and audio scripts. In either cases, it is a customization specialist's responsibility to develop a soundly integrated course using the new content and the original content and to maintain the quality of the course.

 Resources

The new contents are developed based on the customization requirements and design document as resources. Of course, the expertise of SMEs and technical developers is another resource to produce high quality content.

 Products

At the end of this step, finalized course contents are developed including customized original contents and newly developed contents. These contents will be developed in an appropriate format of media in the next step.

INSTRUCTIONAL DELIVERY SYSTEM & MATERIAL DEVELOPMENT

This step includes actual development of required delivery systems and materials, such as configurations of the computer system and software development for CBT and Internet-based instruction, development of overhead projector materials, desktop publishing for print-based materials, and development of audiovisual materials. Those materials can be developed in house or by outside contractors, depending on the regional situation.

 Objectives

Major objectives for developing instructional delivery system and materials are:

- *Produce printed materials including participant's guide (PG), instructor's guide (IG), handouts, overhead projector films, etc.*

The printed material should be produced based on the local practices. For instance, the layout of each page, use of papers, sizes and styles of fonts might be quite different from culture to culture. It is common to use A4-size papers in most countries whereas letter-size papers are used in North America. In some cultures, textbooks are written vertically from right to left, while they are written horizontally from left to right in other cultures.

- *Produce non-print materials such as audio and video tapes, computer software, Internet course homepages, tools, etc.*

Video is another medium which has various video signals in different culture, such as NTSC for most of Asian and American countries and PAL for most of European countries. You should be able to manage the transform the signal of the master tapes. Also, master tapes should be in a high quality for editing and duplication.

For computer software, you have to identify first whether the original and customized software is based on Macintosh or IBM compatible computers as well as the operating systems on which the software is running. If the course is Internet-based, you might want to confirm the speed and available memory of the web server for participants to get logged in and use in a comfortable level of participation. In addition, the design of navigation and down- and up-load of data should be easy for the novice users of the Internet. Development of computer software is much more complex than print materials. The customization specialist should consult computer software designers and programmers in earlier stages of the design and development phases and for further detailed information of development which is not dealt with in this book.

 Activities

Some of the major activities involved in development of instructional delivery system and materials are:

- *Finalize and edit all material contents.*

- *Produce all necessary materials for games, simulations and other instructional activities used in the class.*

- *Develop flowchart for CBT lessons.*

- *Develop storyboard for audio, video, and computer software production.*

- *Produce all required printed materials, audiovisual materials, and computer software, and Internet homepages.*

- *Obtain any necessary copyright clearances.*

Copyright is an important issue to protect intellectual properties. You should identify whether the original material has obtained appropriate copyright for the use in any part of organization or it has limited permission to use.

 Questions

- *What original resources are required to develop the materials, such as original videotape, audio tape, handouts, PG, IG and CBT program?*

- *What are the specifications for each system, such as separate sound tracks of narration and background music for video and audio tapes, and types of source files and authoring tools for CBT programs?*

- *Do you have internal capability to produce required materials? Or who are qualified production vendors in your region?*

 Team

Production specialists for each medium play major roles in this step. The customization specialist should have discussion with them effectively on specific issues from the planning stage for development and production and monitors the entire production process.

 Resources

Translated materials and newly developed contents for the materials are major resources for the instructional system and material development. Also, a list of high quality vendors is a good resource for development.

Products

* *Camera-ready final set of printed and non-printed materials for the course*

* *Storyboard for audio/video/computer software production*

 Continuous Improvement

Edit materials for any possible improvement on translation, new contents, and instructional delivery system and material development. Also, make sure whether each step has been completed as designed in the customization design phase.

CHAPTER 6

Formative Evaluation

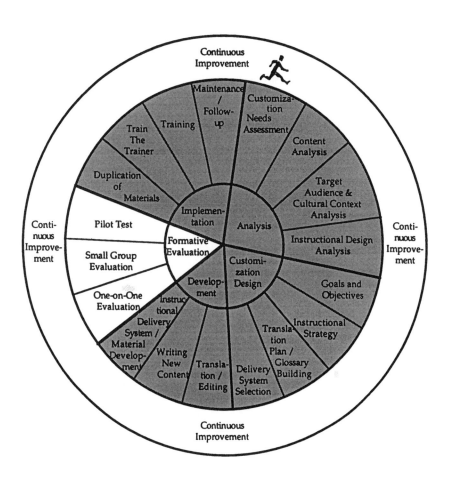

Formative evaluation and revisions should be conducted continuously throughout the entire process of customization in a spirit of continuous improvement. In this formal phase of formative evaluation, three techniques are used. Depending on the local situation, it is the customization specialist's responsibility to utilize the techniques effectively in each phase for producing customized high quality training courses. Although it is usually the case in real projects to conduct a small group evaluation or pilot test only due to the time constraints and participant availability, it is highly recommended to follow all three techniques to ensure the quality of the customized courses.

This phase should be combined with the development phase. You should formatively evaluate your instructional delivery system and materials with sample participants from the target audience and SMEs, while you are developing the materials.

ONE-TO-ONE EVALUATION

It is recommended that the first version of the material is evaluated with two or three participants from the target audience in one-on-one meetings. Any required revisions should be made based on the evaluation results. The sample participants should be able to represent the overall target audience in terms of knowledge and skills they have, learning styles and abilities and culture, and to provide adequate feedback on the instruction.

During the one-on-one meeting for evaluation of materials and instruction, you can discuss various issues generated by the participants and ask questions of participants, which you wanted to clarify in terms of comprehensibility and cultural appropriateness of the course.

In addition, it is difficult to revise audiovisual materials once they are produced. You might want to use audio scripts and video storyboards for one-to-one formative evaluation before you record the audio and shoot the video.

 Objectives

- *Test the customized course with the target audience individually using the materials developed.*

- *Test the instructor's guide with an instructor candidate.*

- *Identify any corrections in content areas, instructional strategy, presentation of instruction, participation activities, and cultural aspects embedded in the course.*

 Activities

- *Review all the materials carefully along with your expected participants and instructors individually.*

- *Determine whether they can easily follow the course, understand the content, achieve the course goals and objectives, and if they feel the course is appropriate in terms of their culture, jobs, etc.*

- *Revise the materials as required.*

 Questions

- *Can a participant follow the instruction easily?*

- *Is the use of language appropriate for him or her?*

- *Does the instructional strategy flow smoothly?*

- *Do all instructional activities appeal to and motivate him or her, and do they enjoy the activities?*

- *Are learning activities culturally appropriate?*

- *Are examples culturally relevant to participants and instructors?*

- *Is the translation of materials easy to understand?*

- *Does he or she achieve the goals and objectives at the appropriate level of evaluation?*

- *Can an instructor follow the instructor's guide easily?*

- *Is there enough time allotted for the course?*

- *What are participants' recommendations for improving learning?*

- *What culturally inappropriate aspects are identified by participants and an instructor?*

- *Do knowledge and skills seem to be easily transferable to the workplace by participants?*

Team

- *Customization specialist*

- *Two or three individuals from the target audience of the course*

- *Instructor candidate*

 Resources

All course materials developed are used in this step.

 Products

After finishing one-to-one evaluation, you should revise the materials reflecting input from participants and an instructor candidate and prepare the revised material for the small group evaluation.

SMALL GROUP EVALUATION

The small group evaluation is conducted with the second version of the materials, which have been revised at the end of the one-to-one evaluation. This is to confirm that the revisions are made appropriately without reflecting any bias of the participants in the one-to-one evaluation. You can also observe and identify group dynamics and common cultural responses in a small group evaluation session. The differences between one-to-one evaluation and small group evaluation are: (1) you do not discuss any issues with participants during the evaluation session, rather you observe the small class, and (2) you evaluate and improve the learning environment as well as individual materials.

 Objectives

Although the context of the evaluation is different from the one-to-one evaluation, the objectives are basically the same as in the one-to-one evaluation.

- *Test the customized course with a small group of the target audience using the revised materials.*

- *Identify and make any corrections.*

Activities

• *Select potential participants and an instructor candidate.*

• *Arrange the learning environment including all required media and materials.*

• *Conduct a pilot class with a small group of participants and an instructor candidate or a master instructor.*

• *Determine how the course flows, whether participants can easily follow the course, understand the content, achieve goals and objectives, and feel the course is appropriate in terms of their culture.*

• *Look for physical cues like body language to understand the reactions of participants towards the course.*

• *Determine whether the instructor has any problems using an instructor's guide and other instructional materials.*

• *Revise the materials as required.*

 Questions

The same questions used for one-to-one evaluation can be asked for small group evaluation. Review them here. In addition, the following questions can be used:

• *Do participants engage in the instructional activities?*

• *Are group activities culturally appropriate?*

• *Are breaks and lunch timed suitable?*

• *Does the instructor's guide help instructor to manage the class?*

• *Do the instructor's guide and participants' guide match each other so that an instructor can facilitate the class effectively and participants can follow the instruction?*

• *Are the audio and video qualities good enough to listen to and watch and comprehend the content?*

Team

The customization specialist observes the small group evaluation session to identify revision points of instruction while an instructor manages the course with the participation of seven or eight people from the target audience. After the class, a discussion session with the instructor and the participants gives an opportunity for the customization specialist to identify participants' feelings and reactions about the course. At this time, ask specific questions about the cultural congruence.

 Resources

Revised materials are used in the small group evaluation as well as other instructional equipment and media.

 Products

After conducting small group evaluation session, the materials should be revised again based on the results of observation and feedback from instructor and participants and will be the products of this step.

PILOT TEST

A pilot test is conducted with the latest version of the instructional materials in a learning environment that is identical to the actual learning environment. It is recommended to have a sizable class in a classroom which will be actually used if the course uses classroom instruction. It is common to use the first class of the actual course as a pilot test. The differences between the small group evaluation and pilot test are: (1) the pilot test is with the actual size of the class and the small group evaluation is with a sample of participants, (2) there is no discussion with participants about the course itself in terms of instructional materials, delivery of instruction, and learning environment after the pilot test, rather participants' feedback is collected through the level 1 evaluation which identifies the participants' reactions on the course in general, (3) since the pilot test is running with the actual size of the class, the participants' behavior and group activities can represent the actual responses of the actual classes which will be implemented according to the implementation plan, and

(4) you can pre-test the implementation plan which you developed in the design phase. While you prepare for the pilot test, you can get cooperation from the administration department for assigning and arranging the classroom, participants' registration, material delivery, instructional equipment installation, participants' transportation and accommodation, etc. This is a good chance to check for the logistics of running the course.

Since computer-based instruction and Internet-based instruction are developed and implemented for individualized learning, conducting several one-to-one evaluations would serve as a pilot test.

 Objectives

The objectives are still the same as one-to-one evaluation and small group evaluation in terms of identifying ineffective, culturally inappropriate aspects of the course. Since the pilot test is your last chance to have formal formative evaluation before the actual courses are running and there will be heavy investment to produce the learning materials massively, the customization specialist should be cautious to gather all necessary improvement information and revise the course.

- *Test the customized course with a group of participants using the revised materials and a master instructor.*

- *Identify any corrections required.*

- *Revise the instructional materials and learning environment and finalize them.*

- *Revise implementation plan to be more effective and efficient reflecting any issues around the actual implementation in the region.*

 Activities

- *Make the necessary arrangements for the pilot test, which is identical to the actual class.*
- *Have the master instructor conduct the class.*
- *Observe the class.*
- *Determine whether the course is conducted as designed.*

- *Identify whether there are other cultural aspects which are not appropriate in the actual size of the class.*

- *Revise the materials and implementation plan as required.*

 Questions

Questions asked in the one-to-one evaluation and small group evaluation are also used in the pilot test. In addition, the following questions can be asked to identify additional revision points of the course:

- *How appropriate is the participants composed culturally in a class, in terms of gender, organizational position, and job?*

- *How appropriate is the class size for the interaction among participants and between the instructor and participants?*

- *How well are all audio materials developed and delivered so that everyone in the class can listen clearly?*

- *How well are the video materials developed and delivered so that everyone can watch clearly in the class?*

- *Does equipment operate perfectly?*

- *How appropriate and similar is the physical classroom environment to participants' workplace if it is one of the requirements?*

- *How well do all instructional activities work with the class grouping?*

- *What are other corrections required in the materials in terms of typographical errors, page layout, print quality, audio and video quality, etc.?*

- *Are all evaluation materials clearly developed without any errors?*

- *Are there any bugs in the computer software?*

 Team

Like with the small group evaluation session, the customization specialist observes the class in which an instructor runs the course with an actual class-size group of participants from the target audience.

Resources

All required materials for the course should be used in this step.

 Products

After the pilot test, the final revision should be completed. The revised materials are the final product of the evaluation phase.

 Continuous Improvement

Although this phase is a formal formative evaluation, you could get useful feedback about the course informally as well. Listen to what people say about the course. Analyze and reflect on the feedback for revision and improvement of the course.

CHAPTER 7

Implementation of Instructional Interventions

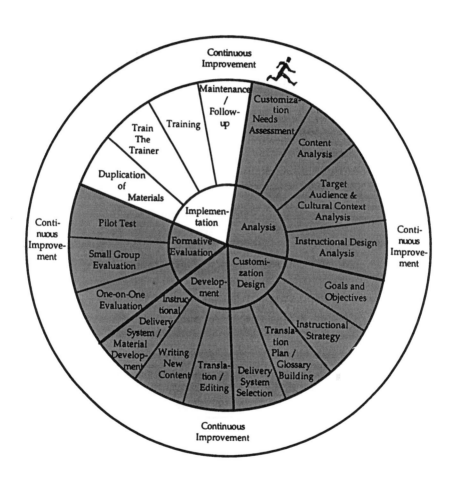

Once you have redesigned, developed, and formatively evaluated the course, the implementation phase for customized courses is identical to other training courses which you have originally developed originally. The steps of this phase include duplication of materials, train-the-trainer, delivery of the course, maintenance, and follow-up.

DUPLICATION OF MATERIALS

 Objectives

- *Duplicate all instructional materials as much as required.*

Considering the number of participants, instructors and classes, an adequate number of materials should be duplicated.

 Activities

- *Produce all necessary audio/video/computer software.*

- *Duplicate all materials in required quantity.*

 Team

The customization specialist is responsible for preparing an adequate number of materials for the course. Actual duplication can be assisted by material production specialists.

  Resources and Products

Finalized materials are duplicated as necessary, using all the camera-ready materials produced in the previous phase.

TRAIN THE TRAINER (TTT)

If the number of participants who take the course is too large for one instructor or facilitator, multiple instructors or facilitators will be required to deliver the course and the adequate number of instructors and facilitators should be trained and qualified for the course delivery. The train-the-trainer session should run as if the course is taking place for the actual participants. In addition to learning the content of the course itself as participants would learn, participants of TTT session should learn how to deliver the course effectively. The TTT participants should achieve the knowledge and skills for using the instructional materials and equipment, facilitating small and large group discussion and other instructional activities, managing class hours and breaks, motivating participants, etc. The TTT session is delivered by a master instructor with the cooperation of the customization specialist. The potential instructors should take the TTT session and be encouraged to incorporate their own experiences related to the objectives of the course and cultural adaptation. It is especially important to note that an instructor's role is critical for adapting the course for cultural congruency during the actual classes.

   If the number of the target audience is small enough and the course requires only one instructor, this step is not necessary and can be skipped.

 Objectives
- *Train and certify instructors.*

 Activities
- *Arrange the learning environment as designed for the course.*

- *Conduct TTT classes as designed and scheduled in the customization design phase.*

- *Discuss any potential cultural adaptation issues with future instructors.*

 Questions
- *Who is a master instructor?*

- *How many instructors does the course require?*

- *What is the appropriate number of participants in a TTT class?*

- *How many classes are required to teach and certify all future instructors of the course?*

Team

A master instructor delivers the course to the instructor candidates as if he or she is running the course for the actual target audiences. He or she also presents teaching directions in the TTT session as designed. A customization specialist helps the master instructor by providing additional information about the course and providing additional tips for cultural adaptation of the course content and delivery. In addition, training administrators are involved for running the TTT sessions.

 Resources

TTT participants should be provided with all materials including instructor's guide and participant's guide, as well as other instructional materials and equipment which will be using in the delivery of the course.

 Products

By completing the TTT sessions, you will have an adequate number of certified instructors.

DELIVERY OF THE COURSE

This step is for conducting the actual classes of the course to train the target audience in your region. The certified instructors deliver the course to the participants using all the materials developed in a designed learning environment.

 Objectives

- *Conduct the training course as designed using all developed materials.*

 Activities

- *Confirm the registration of participants to take the course.*

- *Confirm the schedule of the class with the assigned instructor.*

- *Arrange and check the learning environment as called for.*

- *Open the classes as scheduled.*

- *Monitor if the course is running smoothly as designed.*

- *Collect participants evaluation results.*

 Questions

- *Is the course presented as designed?*

- *Do the instructors deliver the course with confidence?*

- *Is the learning environment well prepared as designed?*

- *Are instructional hardware and software well operated as designed?*

- *Do participants understand the content presented and achieve the course goals and objectives?*

- *What are the evaluation results?*

 Resources

All materials are required to deliver the course by the certified instructors.

MAINTENANCE & FOLLOW-UP

Although the course is delivered to the target audience successfully, there might be some areas in the course which should be revised over time. Look for any defects of the course continuously, analyze the cause of them, and revise the course accordingly. Also, depending on the course, follow-up activities are necessary. For instance, if the course asks participants to submit any assignments after the course has been taken, those assignments should be collected and participants should get feedback on them. To increase the learning and transfer of knowledge and skills acquired in the class to participants' real life and work, it is beneficial to confirm their transfer of learning. Any bottlenecks participants have while they make an effort to transfer the learning in their workplace should be identified and removed to gain the benefits of training courses and to get a profitable return on investment. The transfer of learning in real life is not just a matter of the quality of the course or the achievement level of participants during the class. The work environment and system should support the transfer of learning.

 Objectives

- *Maintain the quality of the course in terms of up-to-date content and cultural appropriateness.*

- *Analyze the results of level 1, 2, 3, and/or 4 evaluations as designed, and revise the course as required.*

- *Continuously improve the course.*

 Activities

- *Monitor the classes.*

- *Monitor instructors' quality of course delivery.*

- *Investigate the course content regularly to be up-to-date.*

- *Revise the course as required.*

- *Monitor participants' performance change and improvement after they return to their workplaces.*

- *Discuss with participants any bottlenecks of transferring the learning into the workplace.*

 Questions

- *Is the content of the course still up-to-date and culturally accordant?*

- *Are instructional environment and instructional delivery system still working well?*

- *Are the media selected cost effective over time?*

- *What are the areas for improvement in terms of instructional strategy?*

- *What are the evaluation results of the course over time?*

- *Do participants show change or improvement of their performance?*

- *What are the comments from participants' bosses, peers, and subordinates on their performance after participants took the course?*

- *What difficulties and bottlenecks do participants have when they try to apply their knowledge and skills acquired in the course to their workplace and life?*

- *Does the organization still have problems or needs which could be resolved through the course?*

- *What can be improved in the course for more effectiveness in terms of course delivery and participants' learning?*

 Team

A customization specialist takes the responsibility to maintain the quality of the course and revise it as required. In addition, he or she is responsible for the follow-up activities. The follow-up activities requires involvement of various stakeholders regarding the course, participants' performance, and organizational performance improvement and change.

 Resources

- *Results from class observations and observations of graduating participants' performance*

- *Input from instructors, participants, subject matter experts, and other stakeholders in the organization*

- *Various evaluation results*

 Products

Through the maintenance and follow-up activities, the quality and effectiveness of the course is kept strongly.

Continuous Improvement

The continuous improvement in the implementation phase is most important for the consistent success of the course. Evaluate the course carefully in many aspects over time as long as the course is offered to the target audience. Watch for the change of trends in the development of subject matter, cultural traits, target audience's characteristics, available technology, feedback about the course from various groups of people, organizational and employees' needs, organizational changes, stakeholders' needs, etc.

PART III

A Case Study of Transcultural Customization

CHAPTER 8

Transcultural Customization of Training Programs in Motorola University

INTRODUCTION

A case study of Motorola, Inc. was conducted to identify practices of the transcultural customization process within a global organization. (This case study was conducted in 1995.) Motorola, Inc. is in the electronics and electrical equipment industry and one of the Fortune global 500 companies (Fortune, 1998). The company is located in over 50 countries with headquarters in the U.S. Major sites include the U.S., China, Hong Kong, Japan, Korea, Malaysia, Singapore, Taiwan, France, Germany, U.K., Canada, Israel, and Mexico. Within Motorola, Inc., Motorola University is the core organization for the training and education of employees while each sector and group of the company has its own training department when this case study was conducted. This study was specifically focused on a case in Motorola University. Motorola University was selected as a case because it is a global organization with many organizational business sites worldwide, and it is well-known for its adaptation and implementation of concepts and process of instructional systems design in its training and education system.

Purpose

The case study was focused on the identification of the current status of practices of transcultural customization of training programs in various regions within Motorola University. The regions in Motorola University were categorized by their geographical locations around the world. At the highest level, there were the Americas, Asia, and European continent-regions managed by directors of each region. Each region was divided into sub-regions which represent a part of a country, a country, or a whole continent, depending on the management strategy and size of the business a sub-region covers.

The specific components, processes, and procedures of a model, which were used in the transcultural customization of training programs as well as the current system for transcultural customization, were identified. In addition, general information was collected regarding the demographics of the company, the training department, and the instructional design model used.

The questions guiding this study were:

1. What are the perceived needs for transcultural customization of training programs by the regions in the organization?

2. What is the current status of instructional design and development in general and transcultural customization in each sub-region of the company as well as in the continental regions?

3. What practices in conducting transcultural customization are being implemented and how effective are they?

4. What are the components and requirements of, and parameters for, a transcultural customization model that would result in its acceptance and use?

5. What is the current system for transcultural customization?

Participants

Twelve participants was interviewed including three directors of each continent-region, a group of training managers, instructional designers, and customization coordinators of sub-regions in Motorola University. Participants were responsible either directly or indirectly for the instructional design and customization of training programs in regions.

Procedure

First, directors, eligible managers, instructional designers, and customization coordinators were identified through one of the managers in the Strategic Education Department in Motorola University located in the mid-west region of the USA. Second, interviews with directors of three continent-regions were conducted to: (a) identify their general perceptions, policies and process on transcultural customization of training programs; and (b) obtain a list of appropriate managers to contact for the research in each continent-region. Third, interviews of managers of sub-regions were conducted. Those managers were in charge of entire sub-regions within a continent-region and reported to the director. Fourth, the instructional designers and customization coordinators, who are responsible for the transcultural customization of training programs, were interviewed. Finally, documents on the instructional design model and transcultural customization system/model used by different regions were reviewed and analyzed by comparing and contrasting them with each other to come up with a common process for transcultural customization.

All interviews were initiated with prepared interview questions. The interview questions were developed around five major questions and are listed as follows:

1. What are the perceived needs for transcultural customization of training programs by the regions in the organization?
   - What would be your reasons for using or offering courses developed in other regions? Required course? Good reputation? Specific needs? Or other?
   - What has been, what is, or what would be your reasons for transcultural customization of instructional courses?
   - Have you heard of any difficulties or complaints from your instructional designers and/or those delivering instructional programs in your region which were developed in other regions? If so, what were the difficulties or complaints they addressed? How did you resolve the problem?
   - Have you heard of any difficulties or complaints from other regions regarding any cultural inappropriateness of your instructional program in their culture?

2. What is the current status of instructional design and development in general and transcultural customization in each sub-region of the company as well as in the continental regions?
   • What is your responsibility regarding instructional programs developed and/or conducted in your region?
   • Do you design and develop any courses to deliver to your local employees in your region? If so, what would be the procedural model for designing and developing instruction?
   • How many people do you have for designing new instructional courses and for delivering instructional courses in your regions?
   • Do you adapt and customize any courses which have been developed in another region to deliver to employees in your region?
   • Is anyone responsible for customizing or making instructional programs culturally appropriate for your region? Do you have any designated full-time customization specialists, instructional designers or trainers in your region?

3. What practices in conducting transcultural customization are being implemented and how effective are they?
   • What kinds of courses do you customize?
   • How many courses have you customized?
   • How would you know if a customized course fits with your culture?
   • What process/procedure do you use for customizing training courses culturally? In your experience with customization projects, how long does the customization process take for a 4-hour course?
   • Do you have a documented process of customization? If so, what is it? If not, what would be the ideal process for customization or adaptation of instructional courses or materials?

4. What are the components and requirements of, and parameters for, a transcultural customization model that would result in its acceptance and use?
   • Who developed the transcultural customization model?
   • How has the model been developed?

- How does the model work for your customization project?
- Has the model been institutionalized in your region for customization projects?

5. What is the current system for transcultural customization?
   - How do you obtain information regarding course availability and the course materials? What processes are involved for that?
   - Who is involved during the customization process?
   - What materials and resources are required for the customization process?
   - Do you have cultural SMEs whom you can consult?
   - Are there people you know who would be good for me to talk with regarding the transcultural customization in detail?

The above questions were modified during the actual interview with the interviewees. The directors and managers were informed of the project's purpose and asked to participate in the interviews by the contact person through e-mail. The instructional designers and/or customization coordinators were contacted after the interviews with managers. Due to the fact that participants are located all around the world, interviews were conducted using the telephone. The actual phone interviews were scheduled ahead of time through e-mail and phone calls. The interview was tape recorded with the interviewees' permission.

The existence of each region's document of instructional design and transcultural customization systems were identified through interviews of managers, instructional designers, and customization specialists. Any available documents were collected by mail and fax. All data, including interview results and documents on each region's instructional design model and transcultural customization system/model, were compared for their common and distinct processes among regions and analyzed to answer the guiding questions. Also, major steps for the process were identified and described.

Table 5 shows interviewees by each region of the organization. It also indicates availability of instructional designer(s) in each region, except the Europe Region. Although there was an instructional designer in the Europe region, she was not interviewed. Each interview was between twenty and fifty minutes in length.

Table 5: Interviewees by Regions of the Company

Continent	Country	Director	Regional Manager	Instructional Designer	Training Administrator
Asia		X			
	China		X	X	
	Japan		X	X	
	Korea		X	X	
Americas		X			
	Latin America		X		X
	US			X (Working on a Latin America Project)	
Europe		X		X (not interviewed)	

The analysis results for current status and process are described in the following categories: (a) perceived needs for transcultural customization of training programs by training professionals in the regions, (b) current practice of instructional design and transcultural customization in the regions, (c) customization process documented in the Asia region, and (d) current system for transcultural customization of training programs.

PERCEIVED NEEDS FOR TRANSCULTURAL CUSTOMIZATION OF TRAINING PROGRAMS

Cultural Differences

The most important challenge for customizing a course is apparent cultural differences in training programs. A director of the Americas region said:

> One of the largest problems is the perception that all of the Latin American countries would have a common culture. And that turns out not to be true. There are some specific cultural areas country by

country. Even though the majority of the countries is Spanish speaking, there are still cultural differences. And in fact, there are also language differences between the countries. The Spanish spoken in Mexico is probably around 15% different from the Spanish spoken in Argentina. And, of course, in Brazil, you have a different language which is Portuguese. From a cultural standpoint, there are cultural differences.

In the Latin America region, a communication problem caused by cultural differences was identified between the central business unit office in the US and a regional office for that business unit. "For instance, in Mexico, you say it will be ready by next Friday. Next Friday is four days after Monday in the same week. But in the US, it's a week after this Friday," said a regional training administrator. Similarly, a regional manager of Latin America also said:

> In Mexico, if they say that they will call you tomorrow, Americans would wait for a phone call the next day. However, Mexicans actually mean that they will call you sometime in the near future. In many cases, translation is not enough to interpret the meaning.

The problems are mainly due to lack of knowledge of different cultures and lack of language skills in each place.

Two projects have been identified in the Latin America region to solve the communication problem and further to develop courses culturally more appropriate for the Latin Americans. One is the investigation of learning preferences of Latin Americans, and the other is the identification of transcultural competencies for effective communication between U.S. Americans and Latin Americans.

An analysis of learning preferences or learning styles of the target audience is an important task in the design of instruction. As the director of the Americas region said, "if the materials rely, for instance, on words, and the learning preference is symbolic, we probably need to be concerned with it." The results of the analysis suggest customization of courses from one culture to another.

It is expected that the results of this project would help in the design and customizing of training programs based on the learning style of the regional target population.

On the other hand, a needs assessment project has been conducted by an instructional designer who is in a U.S. region and bilingual in English and Spanish. The purpose of this project was to look at success stories and opportunities for improvement of communication between US American and Latin American cultures. A dozen engineers and managers in each culture were interviewed by the instructional designer. The main findings include:

1. The communication in general seems positive and has increased in its effectiveness in the last five years,

2. Participants of the project in both cultures perceived cultural differences,

3. Received cultural differences are different between people in different cultures,

4. There are issues around language, and

5. There are listening attitude problems in terms of different perceptions of communication among people speaking different native languages. People tended to listen to other's opinions with their own selected perception rather than try to understand the other's intentions behind the opinions.

As a result of this project, a set of objectives is recommended to develop a training course. This course is to address cultural awareness and cross-cultural communication, organizational structure, and environmental issues. The course is also based on the learning preference findings. The course is under development in Spanish for managers and engineers in Mexico and in English for the managers and engineers in the U.S. This course will be developed in two different languages for the same goals and objectives for the functionally similar, but culturally different, target populations. This course is an experiment in terms of assessing effectiveness of a course developed in different cultures with the same objectives in contrast to a course developed in one culture and customized for a different culture.

Another perceived need for transcultural customization was mentioned by every interviewee: cultural differences appeared in the training materials. Some of the examples are presented in the following section.

Examples of Cultural Differences in the Training Materials

Content of examples. There are many examples from football or baseball in the training materials designed in the US regions. However, Latin Americans are not familiar with those sports. Rather, they like soccer games. In the case of Japanese culture, although people may enjoy soccer games in Japan, it is not their first choice of a favorite sport. A regional manager of China also mentioned cultural differences in the materials:

> There are many cultural differences: Phrases we don't use, references of American games, idioms, and acronyms.

Thus, appropriate modifications of examples are required to enhance the cultural appropriateness of the course for the regional target audience.

Selection of instructional media and strategy. In the case of video materials, the regional manager of Latin America said:

> Sometimes the videotapes are dubbed or captioned. [However] it still doesn't carry the message. For instance, in Mexico, [people] like videotapes. They like movies. But the tapes are in English. Even though sometimes the video has a Spanish caption, it doesn't carry the message. So the intention of using video is lost. So maybe using a case study over video tape might be a better choice. Now an instructional designer has choices to make: (1) a medium is right but language is wrong, and (2) language is right but the medium is wrong.

Use of bullet points. Another example is use of bullet points versus complete sentences. For the use of overhead materials, things have to be in complete sentences for Latin Americans, rather than bullet points which US Americans are used to. In addition, Latin Americans prefer training materials with symbols and figures compared to traditional text-based materials.

Language Differences

Most of the original training programs have been designed and developed in the U.S. in English. When a region other than the U.S. and English speaking countries decides to offer a training program in the region, translation is involved in the customization process. The main languages spoken in the Latin America region are Portuguese for Brazil and Spanish for other countries in the region. However, more specific language differences within the region are reported by the regional training administrator:

> Although many countries in Latin America use Spanish, each country has different ways of communicating in Spanish. So if the materials are translated in Mexico, people in Argentina wouldn't like it. And if Argentina people make translations, then people in Columbia wouldn't like it.

Usually there is only one translation of materials for the whole Latin America region. He mentioned that "content is not a problem usually. Use of language is difficult." After mentioning different language use in Spanish speaking countries in Latin America, he also said, "we have found the most appropriate country in the region for translation is Columbia ." He also mentioned the following as ways to overcome the language differences:

> When we are sending translated materials to a country and we know that the materials are not translated in that country, we make sure to talk to the people in the country to clarify words they don't understand. So when people leave the classroom they can explain what the words mean.
>
> We are also developing a glossary of terms [to explain] how you would say a certain word in Mexico, in Columbia, in Venezuela, and in Chile. So people who deliver the course in different countries can easily identify different words.

Difficulties of translation of materials also come from the societal and cultural differences. The instructional designer for the China region said:

·[One of the difficulties is] inconsistent translation of terms. For instance, translation of marketing terms is difficult, because of different marketing systems between the U.S. and China. We asked a Chinese marketing professor here, but the university curriculum doesn't deal with that content. So I just have to train our translators to be familiar with Motorola terms and American culture.

In fact, a literal translation of language is not sufficient. Materials should be translated to be understood by the target audience in the region, in terms of content, culture, business, and societal background of the region. Translators should be not only experts in both the language of the original course and the local language of the region, but also knowledgeable about cultures in the two countries and in the company.

CURRENT STATUS OF INSTRUCTIONAL DESIGN AND TRANSCULTURAL CUSTOMIZATION IN REGIONS

Asia Region

Asia is a region which gets a lot of attention from the world as a growing market. The Asian region is divided into China, Japan, Korea, and Southeast Asia sub-regions. Most of the training programs in this region are originally designed in the U.S. region. The regional training managers and instructional designers obtain the course materials and have translators translate the materials.

China. China is a recently established region and is the fastest growing region in Asia. As business rapidly grows, the demand for training is also growing rapidly. In a situation with many courses being delivered with limited human resources, there are very few courses developed originally in this region. Rather, "virtually every course is from somewhere else," said the regional manager of China. Training programs are usually brought from the U.S. Thus, there is heavy translation required for every project. "About 90% of the instructional designer's time is for translation and customization," said the regional manager. Most courses are just translated with a little customization. Currently 10 to 12 translation projects are going on. Depending on the subject, the instructional designer adds more explanations in the content to increase the comprehensibility of the materials.

There are three teams for the training function: Design, delivery, and marketing teams. The design team has 4 people who are responsible for translation, instructional design, and language training including English for Chinese employees and Chinese for non-Chinese employees.

Japan. Three instructional designers are working in Japan, including two manager-level personnel. Those two managers were trained in the field of instructional design in the U.S. As an experienced instructional designer, the regional manager helps the local instructional designer who is actually conducting projects, developing his own instructional design knowledge and skills, and understanding the original courses which will be customized for the region.

Currently, fewer than 5% of the courses are designed originally in the region, because, as the regional manager said, "we have a huge bubble of very core English-based courses that we need to convert into Japanese." He also mentioned that, "once that is done, you'll see the local design go up quite a bit, probably 70%."

According to the regional manager, the customization process performed in the region is as follows:

1. obtain the course materials as published;

2. decide whether the course is customizable as it is designed or redesign of the course is required (currently the decision is subjectively made by the manager and instructional designer);

3. analyze characteristics of the local target population;

4. observe the original course taught by a master instructor with a project committee, which consists of usually one person in a practical sense. Ideally, a project committee includes more than three persons including local instructional designer, local SME, translator, and local instructor;

5. develop a customization document for the course;

6. translate/customize the course; and

7. pilot the customized course with the target audience.

This process is similar to the customization process which the China, Japan, and Korea regions developed separately with cooperation of a translation specialist located in the U.S. central office. The customization process is described in a later section of this chapter.

Korea. This region has a customization coordinator as well as a local instructional designer who has an ISD background. The customization coordinator organizes customization projects from the obtaining of course materials from the U.S. region, to contracting translators, and scheduling training classes. This person has an administrative role rather than actual customization design responsibility. The instructional designer is more involved in the customization design work than the customization coordinator.

In terms of evaluation of customized courses, formative evaluation is conducted throughout the process of customization by gathering feedback from SMEs and translators. The first class of a course is used as a pilot test for the course. The translated materials are then used by the target population and a certified instructor. After the class, the participants' feedback regarding the course materials and the course in general is collected to find areas in need of improvement.

This region has developed a course customization process similar to the China and Japan regions. The process is being institutionalized in the regions and has shown an improvement in cycle time and quality of customization. They also developed a standard translator selection process, translation evaluation process, and outside service contract procedure to be used internally. The translation evaluation process focuses on the feedback from the various activities during the customization project, such as feedback from train-the-trainer and pilot sessions.

Southeast Asia. Compared to other Asia regions, the practices of training in this region are different. Training specialists in this region provide consulting services to other business organizations, including customization and delivery of Motorola training programs to other organizations.

Since there is no instructional designer in the region, all courses, which are provided to clients, are developed in other regions in the organization. The customization in this region involves translation of materials, if necessary, and change or deletion of the company name in the materials. Delivery of courses is performed either by Motorola instructors or by the client's instructors who are certified by Motorola, depending on the project contract. The main source of evaluation is feedback from the client in the form of whether they liked the course or not.

Latin America Region

The Latin America region is one of two large sub-regions in the Americas region. The U.S. region, which is the other Americas region, is divided into Central, East, Southwest, West and Hawaii sub-regions. Since this research dealt with national cultural differences rather than cultural differences within a country, an in-depth investigation of the U.S. sub-regions has not been conducted. This research is focused instead on the current status of customization practice in the Latin America region in the Americas as well as other regions around the world. However, it is important to mention that there is an issue of cultural differences among U.S. sub-regions caused by geographical local cultures and among different business units within the organization.

A director for the Americas region, a regional director and a training administrator for the Latin America region were interviewed to gather information about this region.

Background. Compared to U.S. sub-regions and other regions around the world, Latin America is fairly new to the organization. Consequently, this region is "many steps behind the U.S., Asia, and Europe," according to the regional training administrator. There is no instructional designer assigned to this region. There are few contracted translators, and several local instructors who deliver training courses in different Latin American countries including Argentina, Brazil, Chile, Columbia, Costa Rica, Mexico, Puerto Rico, and Venezuela.

In terms of organizational operation in the region, Motorola has major manufacturing facilities in Mexico, Puerto Rico, and Costa Rica. There are local instructors for these countries. The other countries have only sales and service representatives and do not have local instructors.

Status of instructional design, translation, and transcultural customization of training programs. Since there is no instructional designer available for the region, there are no courses originally designed in the region. The current training courses are originally designed and developed in the U.S. regions. Since there is no staff for the instructional design or customization process in the region, the training materials are translated into the local languages, Spanish or

Portuguese, without proper transcultural customization of training programs. Any kind of modification is up to the instructors who deliver the training program to the local audience.

A project for preparing a half-day course takes one or two months for translation by contracted translator(s) who are located either in the U.S. central office or locality. Another one or two months are taken for production in the U.S. The following is the translation process performed in the region, according to the regional training administrator:

1. obtain the training materials from the U.S.;

2. have a subject matter expert (SME) to go through the materials;

3. get local translators, who know Motorola specific terms, to translate the materials;

4. proofread the material to correct technical content; and

5. have linguistic experts to read the translated materials to find any cultural language problems.

This process is explained by the regional training administrator. He mentioned that there is no document regarding translation or customization in the region.

Europe Region

Only an interview with a director of the Europe region was conducted to gather general information regarding current status of instructional design and customization processes in the region.

There is an instructional designer who is based in the United Kingdom. This person is responsible to design and obtain courses for all European countries, such as English, French, and German speaking countries including African and Middle East countries. According to the director of the region, about 70% of the courses in the region come from the U.S. regions. The other 30% are developed locally. Courses are also brought from outside of the company in Europe.

Courses are selected through a product review meeting which is held every four months. Then a training manager and/or an instructional designer attends the train-the-trainer session for the course.

Some of the efforts for making courses more appropriate to the regional target population are: (a) to have European instructors run the courses, and (b) to customize names and examples in the materials. In addition, all training are evaluated with the same process for Kirkpatrick's levels 1 and 2 of evaluation.

Among European countries, only France has a local training manager who is responsible for the courses delivered in French. The director describes the French training manger's responsibility as follows:

> If he has a demand for training, when a course is coming from outside of the country, he monitors translation to have the vocabulary right.

CUSTOMIZATION PROCESS IN ASIA REGION

This section reports the customization process which has been developed and documented in the Asia region. Although China, Japan, and Korea regions separately developed the process, the main process is identical with some minor differences. For each step, process tasks are listed with the expected output, responsible personnel, and contact persons within the organization. The following are the main steps for the customization process and key tasks for each step:

- Source materials: contact the U.S. region to request master copies of course materials;

- Develop project schedule: schedule pilot and/or train-the-trainer session, translation delivery, printing, etc.;

- Form a project team: identify appropriate translator, local SME, instructor candidates;

- Estimate project costs: estimate translation fee and pilot/TTT fee;

- Coordinate English pilot/train-the-trainer session: identify master instructor and instructor candidates, arrange master instructor's visit, and prepare English materials;

- Conduct English pilot/TTT;

- Develop customization document: identify objectives, target audience, customization points, instructional strategies for customization;

- Develop glossary: identify and define key words, phrases and concepts;

- Translate/customize materials: incorporate input from customization document and proofread/edit translated materials;

- Run pilot in local language; and

- Finalize translation after revision.

This process was recently developed in each region with the cooperation of a translation process specialist located in the headquarters in the U.S. As described in the earlier section of this chapter, because of logistical differences in each region, actual implementation and institutionalization of the process is in progress. In addition, it seems the level of implementation of the process is different for each region in Asia.

SUGGESTIONS FOR THE BEST PRACTICE OF TRANSCULTURAL CUSTOMIZATION

This section presents suggestions for the best practice of transcultural customization identified from the interviews, which regional managers and instructional designers obtained through trial and error in the field.

Level of Difficulty for Customization

How easy or difficult a training program can be customized could be determined by the subject matter of the course, design quality and documentation of the original course, availability of customization guidelines for the course, language used for developing the original course, availability of a glossary of terms used in the training materials, and availability of materials in an appropriate format.

Subject matter. If a course is dealing with technical content, it is easier to be translated and customized than a course teaching soft skills. An instructional designer mentioned:

For the semiconductor technology course that I am working on, which is a highly technical course, there are not many difficulties. But for the soft skills, in my experience, since the topic was corporate initiatives, such as career path and individual dignity entitlement, the concepts themselves were hard to be translated rather than the training course itself.

The regional manager of Japan also said:

Probably for software, hardware engineering, and more technical manufacturing courses, you don't have to do very much of customization. You are really working on translation. And once you have a glossary, that becomes really easy. [For courses like] Individual Dignity Entitlement, Uncompromising Integrity, and much of the management stuff, you are going to be in the customization environment almost all the time.

Design of the original course. It is important that the original course is designed and documented well. If the course has a potential to be delivered in more than one country, then the course should be designed for modification and adaptation at the early stage of the course design process. The design document should be complete, include references with a detailed description of course background, and be accessed easily.

On the other hand, instructional design techniques used for developing the original course influence the level of difficulty of customization. The regional manager of Japan explained that:

The more modular that a course is designed, the easier for [instructional designers] to customize. If the examples and content are highly intermixed and fully narrative, it becomes very hard to customize. But if you have examples and exercises very separated and distinct, almost like a little puzzle part, you can take those out and replace something back in very easily.

Availability of customization guidelines for a course. If there are documented guidelines developed by the original designer, then customization of the course is easier than without them. In terms of an understanding of the original course, identification of areas of customization can be facilitated. The customization guidelines include: (a) course goals and objectives; (b) parts of the course which should be kept as designed and which can be modified; (c) rationale for a case study, examples and other instructional strategies used in the course; and (d) alternative instructional strategies and examples.

Language. If the language of the region is different from that of the original course, language becomes an important factor for customization. For an easy translation process, use of simple language in the original course material is important. Slang, idioms, and acronyms should be avoided. In addition, use of trained, experienced translators who know the organization and local culture is critical.

Availability of glossary of terms used in the training material. In many cases, terms are used differently depending on the context. A glossary of terms with operational definitions used in the material would help the translation process.

Availability of materials in an appropriate format. The original course materials should be developed in a way that the regional offices can convert them easily into the local system. For instance, with video materials, audio tracks should be separately recorded for the narration and background sound effects so that the local office can easily dub the narration track in the local language. In addition, a script of narration should be provided along with the video tape. The video tape itself should be provided in a high quality format. For instance, use of U-matic or Betacam tapes makes better quality video than use of VHS tapes.

Areas of Customization

Depending on the course to be customized, there are certain things which have to be preserved as designed, such as goals and objectives of the course. If goals and objectives of a course are changed, the course is a new course rather than a customized course. The director of the Americas mentioned:

> It's a program, for instance, intended to relay certain Motorola wide messages. And those Motorola wide messages may not necessarily be absolutely in accord with what you normally find in the [local] culture, yet those are the messages we want to relay. Somehow the

people customizing [the course] have to recognize it. And I think that's one of the things that gets us in trouble. And that's even true in customization here in the U.S. There is a particular process we want to move across Motorola. Then somehow there's got to be some indication of that, when the material is designed, this piece is not to be changed. You can change examples. And you can change how you present it. But the message needs to remain the same.

The regional manager of Japan provided an example:

We try to build some kind of habit in the company consistently across all cultures. That would be a ground to say, 'don't change.' One of those [habits] is a face-to-face dialog in Individual Dignity Entitlement. That is an activity we want everybody to do. So we wouldn't take that kind of [activity] out of the course, because that's a behavior really part of the objective.

The areas which can and cannot be customized should be identified before the actual customization. When those decisions are provided in customization guidelines for a course, the customization can be conducted correctly without losing the purpose of the original course.

CURRENT SYSTEM FOR TRANSCULTURAL CUSTOMIZATION

A traditional instructional design process has been used to design and develop training programs by many instructional designers in the organization. An instructional designer said that "the Dick and Carey model (Dick & Carey, 1990) is a kind of bible to MU instructional designers to follow."

Many courses are developed in the U.S. regions with cooperation of other regions outside of the U.S. For instance, a hard skill course is being designed in one of the U.S. regions and will be pilot-tested in France. The course will be delivered in English using English materials for the pilot test and train-the-trainer session. Eventually, the course will be delivered in French to the target population using English materials.

There is a documented standard process for the global development and launching of training programs in the organization. This process suggests instructional designers obtain regional input from the Analysis to the Evaluation phases of the ISD process for the development of training programs.

However, this process has not yet been implemented fully by the instructional designers in the organization. For instance, the instructional designer in one of the U.S. regions mentioned that she had not contacted other regional personnel for course design. Conversely, she had not been contacted by any instructional designers from other regions concerning the cooperation of designing and developing a course. In addition, the training manager of Korea said, "the process itself is a very powerful tool to develop a course for worldwide delivery. But I have never heard that someone has developed or is developing a course based on the process." Thus, it is up to instructional designers for designing instructional interventions based on one's experiences and competencies.

SUMMARY

Current Status for Transcultural Customization of Training Programs in the Organization

As the regional manager of Japan mentioned, "customization has got to occur in the country of delivery." According to the director of the Americas region, there is no transcultural customization process in place in the organization:

> I don't think there's any process in place in any regions. There's a translation process and perhaps a process for identifying some of the cultural issues. But in terms of actual adaptation of materials, there's a general review kind of process established. But, [for] actual tasks of doing it, I don't believe there's a defined process.

Although the Asia region developed a customization process, the process has not been implemented in the region. The instructional designer of Japan mention that he cannot follow all the steps in terms of the documentation of the process because of time constraints and many on-going projects.

Only a few regions have the capability to design locally originating courses mainly because of high demand of translation for English versions of core courses developed in the U.S., a lack of instructional designers, and a lack of other human resources and budget.

All regions are conducting level 1 evaluation and some regions are conducting level 2 and 3 evaluations for the training programs (see Kirkpatrick (1994) for 4 levels of evaluation).

In most regions, local training specialists, such as instructional designers, training administrators, instructors, and subject matter experts provide knowledge and skills related to local culture. In many cases, if a course is not customized and delivered by a local instructor with translated materials, the transcultural customization of the course is conducted by the instructor.

Common Findings from Regions

The following is a summary of commonly mentioned opinions by several interviewees from different regions:

- Customization should be conducted locally in the region where the course is delivered. In addition, customization projects should be managed by local customization specialists.

- If a local instructor has the role of a customization specialist, he/she should be trained in terms of cultural modification of the course. The instructor should be flexible and spontaneous in responding to the requests of the target audience. If there is not enough staff for customization projects in a region, it might be most practical for that instructor to be the customization specialist.

- It is important to develop and use a glossary for each course to communicate the content of the material better between regions.

- Use of well-trained translators is important.

- Common targets for transcultural customization of training programs are examples and instructional strategies.

- Some important factors for customization are learning styles of target audiences and a well-designed original course with enough background information and design documentation.

- When the original course is designed to be customized easily, the project time for the customization process can be reduced.

References

Abbott, J. (1988). The multicultural workforce: New challenges for trainers. *Training and Development Journal, 42* (8), 12-13.

Andrews, D. H., & Goodson, L. A. (1991). A comparative analysis of models of instructional design. In G. J. Anglin (Ed.), *Instructional technology: Past, present, and future* (pp. 133-155). Englewood, CO: Libraries Unlimited, Inc.

Association for Educational Communications and Technology (1977). *Educational technology: Definition and glossary of terms.* Washington, DC: Association for Educational Communications and Technology.

Bennett, M. J. (1986). Toward ethnorelativism: A developmental model of intercultural sensitivity. In R. M. Paige (Ed.), *Cross-cultural orientation: New conceptualizations and applications.* Lanham, MD: University Press of America.

Bhola, H. S. (1990). 'Words of wisdom' for youth and adults: The cultural context of program design. Paper presented at the World Conference on Education for All, Jomtien, Thailand. ED 319 986.

Dick, W., & Carey, L. (1990). *The systematic design of instruction. (3rd ed.).* New York: Harper Collins Publishers.

Dick, W., & Carey, L. (1996). *The systematic design of instruction. (4th ed.).* New York: Harper Collins Publishers.

Drucker, P. F. (1994). The age of social transformation. *The Atlantic Monthly,* (11), 53-80.

Ely, D. P. (1983). The use of educational communication media in different cultures. *Educational Media International, 20* (1), 12-16.

Ely, D. P. (1989a). Protocols and processes for promoting interactive cross-cultural media transfer. *Educational Media International, 26* (1), 7-12.

Ely, D. P. (1989b). The diffusion of educational technology in Indonesia: A multi-faceted approach. *British Journal of Educational Technology, 20* (3), 183-190.

Ely, D. P. (1990). Portability: Cross-cultural educational perspectives. *Journal of Research on Computing Education, 23*, 272-283.

Gannon, M. J. (1994). *Understanding global cultures: metaphorical journeys through 17 countries.* Thousand Oaks, CA: Sage Publications.

Gustafson, K. L., & Powell, G. C. (1991). Survey of instructional development models with an annotated ERIC bibliography. ED 335 027

Gustafson, K. L., & Tillman, M. H. (1991). Introduction. In L. J. Briggs, K. L. Gustafson, & M. H. Tillman (Eds.). *Instructional design: Principles and applications* (2nd ed., pp. 3-16). Englewood Cliffs, NJ: Educational Technology Publications.

Hall, E. T., & Hall, M. R. (1990). *Understanding cultural differences.* Yarmouth, ME: Intercultural Press, Inc.

Hannum, W., & Hansen, C. (1992). *Instructional systems development in large organizations.* Englewood Cliffs, NJ: Educational Technology Publications.

Hites, J. M. (1991). The design and delivery of training for international students: A case study. ED 333 169.

Hofstede, G. (1980). Motivation, leadership, and organization: Do American theories apply abroad? *Organizational Dynamics, 9* (1), 42-63.

Hofstede, G. (1993). Cultural constraints in management theories. *Academy of Management Executive, 7* (1), 81-94.

Kaplan, A. (1964). *The conduct of inquiry: Methodology for behavioral science.* San Francisco: Chandler Publishing Company.

Kaufman, R. (1992). *Strategic planning plus.* Newbury Park, CA: Sage Publications.

Keller, J. M. (1987a). Strategies for stimulating the motivation to learn. *Performance and Instruction, 26* (10), 1-7.

Keller, J. M. (1987b). The systematic process of motivational design. *Performance and Instruction, 26* (11), 1-7.

King, D. S. (1994). *Development of a formative evaluation model for instructor-led courses.* Unpublished doctoral dissertation, Florida State University, Tallahassee.

Kirkpatrick, D. L. (1994). *Evaluating training programs: The four levels.* San Francisco: Berrett-Koehler

Kolb, D. A. (1976). *Learning style inventory technical manual.* Boston, MA: McBer & Company.

Lynton & Pareek. (1990). Overview of the training process. *Training for development.* West Hartford, CT: Kumarian Press.

Mager, R. F. (1988). *Making instruction work.* Belmont, CA: Lake Publishing Company.

Marquardt, M., & Reynolds, A. (1994). *The global learning organization.* Burr Ridge, IL: Irwin, Inc.

McAlpine, L. (1992). Cross-cultural instructional design: Using the cultural expert to formatively evaluate process and product. *Educational and Training Technology International, 29,* 310-315.

Morical, K., & Tsai, B. (1992). Adapting training for other cultures. *Training and Development, 46* (4), 65-68.

Motorola. (1993). Transcultural competence. [Participant's Guide]. Schaumburg, IL: Author.

O'Hara-Devereaux, M., & Johansen, R. (1994). *Globalwork: Bridging distance, culture, and time.* San Francisco: Jossey-Bass Publishers.

Pettersson, R. (1982). Cultural differences in the perception of image and color in pictures. *Educational Communication and Technology Journal,* 30 (1), 43-53.

Reiser, R. A. (1987). Instructional technology: A history. In R. M. Gagne (Ed.), *Instructional technology: Foundations* (pp. 11-48). Hillsdale, NJ: Lawrence Ealbaum Associated, Publishers.

Reynolds, A. (1990). Training that travels well. *Training and Development, 44* (9), 73-78.

Richey, R. C. (1986). *Theoretical and conceptual bases of instructional design.* New York: Nichols Publishing.

Romiszowski, A. J. (1981). *Designing instructional systems.* New York: Nichols Publishing.

Rothwell, W. J., & Kazanas, H. C. (1992). *Mastering the instructional design process: A systematic approach.* San Francisco: Jossey-Bass Publishers.

Thiagarajan, S. (1988). Performance technology in multicultural environments: Making sense out of contradictory conceptualizations. *Performance & Instruction, 27* (7), 14-16.

Treffman, S. A. (1978). The development of training in organizations. Paper presented at the National Workshop on Extension Staff Development, New Orleans, LA.

Trollip, S. R., & Brown, G. (1987). Designing software for easy translation into other languages. *Journal of Computer-Based Instruction, 14* (3), 119-123.

Trompenaars, F. (1993). *Riding the waves of culture: Understanding cultural diversity in business.* London: The Economist Books.

Zintel, D. (1995). Going global: Designing training for multicultural learners. National Society for Performance and Instruction National Convention Workshop material. Gilroy, CA: The Training Alliance, Inc.

Index

operating system, 88
organizational needs, , 46
organizational strategy

participants:
  sample, 92
  guide, 95
performance technology, 7
physical conditions of facilities, 72
physical cues, 95
pilot class, 95
pilot test, 96, 122
portability, 25
power distance, 16
prerequisites, 54, 55, 56
print-based material, 73, 87
production department, 38
production specialist, 38, 89
products, 11, 37
promotion plan, 78

questions, 11, 37

region management, 51
reinforcement, 21
relevance of content, , 60
resources, 11, 37
roles, 11

small group evaluation, 94
strategic decision, 49
subject matter, 127
subject matter expert, 33, 38.
  local, 33, 38, 56, 57, 84
survey, 61
systems approach, 31

target audience analysis, 57, 122

team, 37
team members, 37
technical developer, 38, 87
technology transfer, 54
train-the-trainer, 48, 102
training:
  administration, 78, 97
  administrator, 38
  specialist, 132
  purpose of, 4
transcultural, 8, 30.
  transfer, 24
  of instructional interventions, 8
transcultural customization, 9, 31, 127.
  model, 35
    emphasis of , 10
    needs for, 10
    outcome of, 10
  process, 13
  need for, 118
transfer of instruction, 9
transfer of learning, 4, 105
transferability of learning outcome, 74
translated material, 55, 120, 123
translation, 84, 117, 120, 121, 123.
glossary, 77
  guidelines, 77, 82
  plan, 80, 82
  process, 77, 125
  requirements, 77
  accuracy of, 84
  quality of, 85
translator, 38, 84, 121, 132

video material, 73, 119, 129
video signal, 88